Oliver Goldsmith

Oliver Goldsmith

Edited by GEORGE PIERCE BAKER

Introduction by AUSTIN DOBSON

A MERMAID DRAMABOOK

HILL AND WANG • NEW YORK

Library of Congress Catalog Card Number: 57-7897

FIRST DRAMABOOK PRINTING MARCH 1958
SECOND PRINTING JANUARY 1964
THIRD PRINTING APRIL 1966
FOURTH PRINTING JUNE 1968

Manufactured in the United States of America
by The Colonial Press Inc.

CONTENTS

	PAGE
Biography	7
Introduction	11
The Good Natur'd Man	27
An Essay on the Theatre	97
A Register of Scotch Marriages	103
She Stoops to Conquer	109

BIOGRAPHY

ACCORDING to the generally accepted account, Oliver Goldsmith was born on the 10th November, 1728, at Pallas, or Pallasmore, in County Longford, Ireland; but it has also been contended that the place of his nativity was Smith Hill-House, Elphin, Roscommon, the residence of his maternal grandfather, the Rev. Oliver Jones, master of the Elphin diocesan school. He was the second son of the Rev. Charles Goldsmith, who, at the time of Oliver's birth, was acting as assistant to Mr. Green, Rector of Kilkenny West. When, in 1730, Mr. Green died, Charles Goldsmith became Rector in his stead, and removed to the hamlet of Lissoy in Westmeath, on the road from Ballymahon to Athlone. Here Oliver passed his childhood. As a boy he was said to be strong and athletic, but dull and thick-witted. He had, however, a marked liking for legends and balladry—tastes which his first schoolmaster, Thomas Byrne, a roving, romancing old soldier of Queen Anne, seems to have fostered to the full. From this preceptor, he passed to other teachers—at Elphin, at Athlone, at Edgeworthstown; but without arousing any special suspicions of his genius. In June, 1744, he went, much against his will, to Trinity College, Dublin, as a sizar or poor scholar. His academic career was not distinguished. He became involved in a college riot. He gave a mixed party in his rooms, and was, in consequence, knocked down by his angry tutor. Thereupon he ran away. His elder brother persuaded him to return to his forgiving Alma Mater, where, on the 27th February, 1749, he took his degree. The only record of his residence at the University is his name scratched on a window-pane: the only tradition, that he wrote songs for street singers, and stole out at night to hear them sung.

By this time his father was dead, and his mother left without means. What was to be his calling? The Church was the first thought. But either from insufficient knowledge, or eccentricity of costume, he was rejected for ordination by the Bishop of Elphin. He tried tutoring. Then he set out to learn law in London, and lost his funds to a Dublin sharper. Eventually, with a view to study medicine, he succeeded in arriving at Edinburgh, whence, in 1754, he migrated to Leyden. A year later, he set out upon a walking tour through France, Germany, Switzerland, and Italy, playing the flute and disputing at convents or universities for food and lodging. In February, 1756, he landed at Dover "with a few half-pence" in his pocket. He was then seven and twenty.

For the next three years his experiences were equally varied. He was successively an apothecary's journeyman on Fish Street Hill; a poor physician (with a dubious diploma) in Southwark; a corrector of the press to Samuel Richardson; and an usher in a Peckham school. From this last employment he drifted to literature-of-all-work under Ralph Griffiths of the *Monthly Review*, with whom he speedily fell out. Then, in February, 1758, appeared his first book, a translation of the *Memoirs* of Jean Marteilhe of Bergerac, a Protestant who had been "condemned to the Galleys of France for his religion." But he was soon back again at Peckham, waiting vaguely for a medical appointment to a factory at Coromandel, which he did not obtain. Finally he was rejected at Surgeons' Hall in December, 1758, as "not qualified for a [ship's] hospital mate." At this period he was living miserably in a little court off Ludgate Hill, and writing a high-sounding *Enquiry into the Present State of Polite Learning in Europe*. The *Enquiry* was published in April, 1759, with some success. From October to November in the same year, he issued *The Bee*, a miscellaneous collection of papers in prose and verse. This brought him to the notice of Smollett; of John Newbery, the bookseller; and (in all probability) of Johnson. Smollett enlisted him for the *British Magazine*; and for Newbery's *Public Ledger* he began, in January, 1760, the series of Chinese Letters afterwards collected (1762) as the *Citizen of the World*. In May, 1761, he was visited by Johnson at the new lodgings into which he had moved at 6 Wine Office Court, Fleet Street.

Henceforth his record is one of hack-work interspersed with masterpieces. He edited the *Lady's Magazine*, for which he wrote *Memoirs of Voltaire*; he also wrote a *History of Mecklenburgh*, 1762; a *Life of Nash*, 1762; and a *History of England* (in letters), 1764. In December, 1764, appeared his famous poem, *The Traveller*, and in the following year, his *Essays*. To these, in 1766, succeeded his solitary novel, the *Vicar of Wakefield*. Two years subsequently, after a fresh course of compilations, he produced at Covent Garden Theatre (29 January, 1768) his comedy of the *Good Natur'd Man*, of which the success was sufficient to justify him in moving to rooms at 2 Brick Court, Middle Temple. Escaping again from historical drudgery, he issued a second poem, *The Deserted Village* (26 May, 1770); and, in rather less than three years more, he crowned his achievements with the comedy of *She Stoops to Conquer*, produced at Covent Garden, 15 March, 1773. This next year he died at Brick Court, 4 April, 1774, and was buried five days later in the burial ground of the Temple Church. In 1776 a monument, with a medallion by Joseph Nollekens, was erected to his memory by the Literary Club, in the south transept of Westminster Abbey. The epitaph, by Johnson, contains the famous *"Nullum quod tetigit non ornavit."* After Goldsmith's death were published his poems of *Retaliation* (1774), the *Haunch of Venison* (1776), and some other minor pieces. In 1801, Bishop Percy brought out a four volume edition of his *Miscellaneous Works*, with a Memoir which constitutes the first source of his biography. An elaborate *Life* followed in 1837 by Mr. (afterwards Sir James) Prior. But this was practically superseded in 1848 by the more authoritative record of John Forster. A delightful summary of Forster's book was prepared in 1849 by Washington Irving, and there are other and more recent memoirs.

INTRODUCTION

WHEN, at the beginning of 1756, Oliver Goldsmith returned from those desultory wanderings on the Continent with which he had been completing an undesigned apprenticeship to authorcraft, it is manifest that, even at the age of seven and twenty, he was still ignorant of his true vocation, since it was only after he had unsuccessfully essayed several other callings that he finally drifted into literature. But it is worthy of note that he seems to have been early attracted to the stage. There is a popular rumour that, very soon after his arrival in England, he figured as a stroller; and it has been suspected, from hints he dropped in later life, that at some time he had actually enacted that multifarious part of "Scrub" in Farquhar's *Beaux' Stratagem* which fascinated even the brilliant Fanny Abington. *The Adventures of a Strolling Player* in the *British Magazine* suggest personal experiences, and again with Farquhar, as the *rôle* taken by Goldsmith's shabby hero is that of Sir Harry Wildair in the *Constant Couple*. Then the account of George Primrose in the *Vicar* has also its theatrical episodes; and George Primrose has always been more or less identified with Goldsmith himself. Lastly, there is a fairly authenticated story that, when he was employed as corrector of the press to Richardson, he had gone so far as to compose a tragedy. He called one morning upon an Edinburgh friend, at that time in London, and from pockets bulging with papers, like those of the Poet in Garrick's farce of *Lethe*, produced a manuscript which he forthwith proceeded to read, hastily blotting everything to which his listener objected. At last he let out that he had already consulted the author of *Clarissa*, whereupon his friend, naturally distrustful of his personal judgment in so critical a case, positively declined to express any further opinion, good or bad. And with that the tragedy disappears from Goldsmith's history. Whether he burned it, as his predecessor Steele burned the play he wrote at Oxford, has not been recorded. In all likelihood it was modelled upon Voltaire, whom he greatly admired; and probably reached no higher level than that of Murphy's *Orphan of China*, or the *Zobeide* of his later friend, Mr. Joseph Cradock of Gumley, to which he was to supply a pleasant Prologue. Both *Zobeide* and the *Orphan* owed their origin to Voltaire, and both were failures. Goldsmith was abler than either of the writers named; but it may safely be postulated that his genius was better suited to Comedy than Tragedy. In any case, although his subsequent writings show him to have been an exceptionally capable and common-sense critic of plays and players, a period of ten years was allowed to elapse before we hear of his next dramatic effort, *The Good Natur'd Man*.

The comedy of the *Good Natur'd Man* was produced at Covent Garden Theatre in January, 1768. It is scarcely necessary, as a preliminary to Goldsmith's plays, to recount the history of the English stage in the Eighteenth Century. That it was not a very illustrious epoch in our theatrical annals is generally admitted. The great Comic Dramatists of the Restoration had passed away, and with them had gone their atmosphere and environment. Those who succeeded to them were inferior artists, working under different conditions, for a different public. The genius of Steele, whose sense of humour was as keen as his perception of character, was not fundamentally dramatic, and he was hampered, moreover, by his genuine and praiseworthy desire to "moralise his song" in accordance with the precepts of the Nonjuror, Jeremy Collier—a desire which, if it prospered in one way, was fated to failure in another. Fielding, who followed, with greater genius and a richer endowment of invention, ruined himself by his reckless return to the old "wit-traps" of Wycherley and Congreve, as well as by his prodigal dispersal, over a dozen hasty and hand-to-mouth performances, of powers which, discreetly combined and controlled, might have crystallised into masterpieces; and his most durable efforts are his mock-heroic burlesques, and his imitations of Regnard and Molière. After these two, either in time or merit—and it is sufficient here to speak of Comedy alone—come the Cibbers, the Murphys, the Footes, the Colmans, the Macklins, the Garricks—all of whom produced acting plays which achieved a fugitive popularity. But Murphy's *Upholsterer*, 1758; Foote's *Minor*, 1760; Colman's *Jealous Wife*, 1761; Macklin's *Man of the World*, 1764-81,[1] and the rest, however applauded in their own day, have not found more than timid and tentative reproduction in ours;

[1] First acted as *The True-born Scotchman*.

and, save with theatrical enthusiasts, have not taken rank
as dramatic literature. They had, notwithstanding, at least
this in their favour, that their tone was far less objection-
able than that of their more gifted forerunners "of the
last age"; and the stage they filled, if scarcely as brilliant,
was certainly cleaner than the stage of the dramatists of
the Caroline era.

One of the causes which, towards the middle of the
Eighteenth Century, tended to impoverish the repertory
of the theatre was the sudden birth and growth of the
Novel. Not only did it convert spectators into readers; but
the sentiment of Richardson leavened and coloured the
labours of the native playwrights, already sobered by the
sermonising of Steele, and controlled by the restrictions
of the Licensing Act which, in 1737, followed Fielding's
Historical Register. Passing then across the Channel, the
new fashion of fiction helped, in the more congenial soil
of France, to develop the *drame sérieux* or *comédie bour-
geoise* which had been inaugurated by that *Préjugé à la
mode* of Nivelle de la Chaussée, afterwards transplanted
to England as Murphy's *Way to Keep Him*. Under the
influence of *Pamela* and *Clarissa*, the *drame sérieux*, modi-
fied and extended by La Chaussée himself, and then by
Diderot and Sedaine, became the *comédie mixte*, and
finally the *comédie larmoyante*—from which last *genre*
comic situation had virtually disappeared, while the object
aimed at was the commending of goodness and virtue
rather than the ridicule of vice and folly. Under the title
of "genteel" or "sentimental" comedy, this new manner
was speedily imported into England, where it flourished,
or endeavoured to flourish, concurrently with such sur-
vivals of the elder manner as still, at Drury Lane and
Covent Garden, struggled for existence against the popularity of pantomime and the cheap resurrection of old
plays. But although it had its vogue and supporters, there
were still those who clung obstinately to the traditions
of the past, and strove, however hopelessly, to sustain a
comic art which should include the element of comedy.
Of such was the *Jealous Wife* of Colman, and even more
conspicuously, the *Clandestine Marriage* which he wrote
with Garrick upon a hint from the first scene of Hogarth's
Marriage à la mode.

That Goldsmith, notwithstanding his first attempt at
Tragedy, would not be found on the side of the sentimen-

talists may perhaps be anticipated. Already, as an obscure
and unknown outsider, he had bitterly resented—like
Fielding before him—that accusation of "lowness" with
which the superfine advocates of gentility sought to stifle
the true function of Comedy as defined by Aristotle. "By
the power of one single monosyllable"—he had written in
the *Present State of Polite Learning*[2]—"our critics have
almost got the victory over humour amongst us. Does the
poet paint the absurdities of the vulgar; then he is *low;*
does he exaggerate the features of folly, to render it more
thoroughly ridiculous, he is then very *low*. In short, they
have proscribed the comic or satyrical muse from every
walk but high life, which, though abounding in fools as
well as the humblest station, is by no means so fruitful in
absurdity. Among well-bred fools we may despise much,
but have little to laugh at; nature seems to present us with
an universal blank of silk, ribbands, smiles and whispers;
absurdity is the poet's game, and good breeding is the nice
concealment of absurdities." In later years—even after his
first play had been brought out—his cry is still the same.
"Humour at present seems to be departing from the Stage,
and it will soon happen that our Comic Players will have
nothing left for it but a fine Coat and a Song. It depends
upon the Audience whether they will actually drive these
poor Merry Creatures from the Stage or sit at a Play as
gloomy as at the Tabernacle"—(*i.e.*, Whitefield's Tabernacle in Tottenham Court Road). In the same paper he
characterises and criticises the new species of dramatic
composition prevailing "under the name of *Sentimental*
Comedy, in which the virtues of Private Life are exhibited,
rather than the Vices exposed, and the Distresses rather
than the Faults of Mankind make our interest in the
piece." He contends that there has been change without
improvement; that the primary purpose of Comedy is to
render folly or vice ridiculous; that humour is of its
essence; and that nothing is gained when it invades the
province of Tragedy. Finally, he felicitously defines sentimental comedy as a "kind of *mulish* production, with all
the defects of its opposite parents, and marked with sterility." "If we are permitted to make Comedy weep," he
argues, "we have an equal right to make Tragedy laugh,
and to set down in Blank Verse the Jests and Repartees of
all the Attendants in a Funeral Procession." These observa-

[2] 1759, p. 154.

tions, as already stated, come from a paper which belongs to a date subsequent to the production of the *Good Natur'd Man*. As a matter of fact, it was contributed by Goldsmith to the *Westminster Magazine*[3] just before the appearance of *She Stoops to Conquer*. But whenever written, his words embody, accurately enough, the characteristics of the new fashion of stage presentment which had risen up to rival the mirth-making efforts of Vanbrugh and Farquhar.

It was in 1766—the year of the publication of the *Vicar of Wakefield*—that Goldsmith set to work upon the *Good Natur'd Man*, his own practical and individual protest against the existing order of things; and the proximate cause of his attempt seems to have been the production by Garrick and Colman of the before-mentioned *Clandestine Marriage*, in which there were distinct indications, particularly in the finished character of Lord Ogleby, a superannuated fop and fine gentleman, that what he regarded as the older and better fashion of writing was not entirely extinguished. The favour with which the *Clandestine Marriage* was received at Drury Lane seemed to augur well for a reaction against "*serious*" comedy; and animated by this hope, Goldsmith set to work upon a piece aiming chiefly at the delineation of character, and the attainment of nature and humour. During 1766 he laboured at it assiduously in the intervals of his other tasks; and he completed it early in the following year. His friends approved it; and Johnson undertook to supply a Prologue. The next thing was to have it played; and this, as the author too well knew, involved "a process truly chymical." It had, in his own words, to be "tried in the manager's fire, strained through a licenser, and purified in the Review, or the newspaper of the day."

This quotation is taken from the *Present State of Polite Learning*,[4] where, unfortunately, he had also printed several other highly injudicious things with respect to the terrible despotism of the monarchs of the stage, the overprominence of that "histrionic Dæmon," the actor, and the cheese-paring policy of vamping-up old pieces to save the expense of "author's nights." These strictures had been anything but grateful to the all-powerful Garrick, who had shewn his sense of them by declining to give his vote to

[3] December, 1772, Vol. I, p. 4.
[4] 1759, pp. 161-2.

Goldsmith when he was a candidate for the secretaryship
at the Royal Academy. For the time being, however,
owing to the death of John Rich, the archadvocate of
pantomime, the affairs of Covent Garden Theatre were in
confusion; and Goldsmith had no option but to offer his
work to the rival manager of Drury Lane. An interview
between Goldsmith and Garrick was accordingly brought
about by Reynolds. Goldsmith was anxious and important:
Garrick ceremonious but cold. The result was a not very
precise understanding that the play should be brought out.
But thereupon followed delays. It is probable that, apart
from his grudge against the author, Garrick was really not
impressed with the piece itself; and it seems that he privately conveyed, both to Johnson and Sir Joshua, his con-
viction that it would not succeed. In the meanwhile, time
passed, and with it the theatrical season. Money, upon
which Goldsmith had counted, was naturally an object to
him; and, unfortunately, while the matter was still in debate, he was obliged to petition Garrick for an advance
upon a note of Francis Newbery. The required advance
was of course granted by the politic manager. As a matter
of course also, it enabled Garrick to make, with greater
confidence, certain suggestions for alterations in the play
which, as may be supposed, were not to the taste of the
author. This brought about a proposal on Garrick's part
for referring the case to the arbitration of William White-
head, the laureate, a mediocre poet who had occasionally
acted as his reader, but who was not, in any sense, an authority upon whose final judgment Goldsmith could rea-
sonably be expected to rely. A scene of so much acrimony
and irritation ensued that the good offices of both Burke
and Reynolds had to be invoked in order to restore peace.

At this juncture, George Colman, Garrick's collaborator
in the *Clandestine Marriage*, became one of the patentees
of Covent Garden Theatre, and Goldsmith promptly offered him the *Good Natur'd Man*. Receiving an encour-
aging reply, he reported to Garrick what he had done, and
Garrick frigidly acquiesced. This was in July, 1767, too
late to produce the play until Christmas. In the interval
new impediments arose. Garrick, already in hot competi-
tion with Covent Garden, and naturally not greatly prepossessed in favour of its latest dramatic recruit, put forward a certain Hugh Kelly with an out and out sentimental
comedy entitled *False Delicacy*. Becoming subsequently

reconciled to Colman, he contrived to secure a tacit under-standing that Goldsmith's play should not be produced until Kelly's piece had enjoyed a preliminary run. Then, putting into force all his administrative tact and finesse, the astute manager of Drury Lane set himself to ensure a favourable reception for *False Delicacy*. The result was that Kelly's washy comedy, equipped with a prologue and epilogue by Garrick, and admirably acted in two of its parts by King and Mrs. Dancer, was brought out trium-phantly on the 23rd January, 1768, ran for eight nights successively, sold vigorously in book form, procured all kinds of adventitious honours for its author, and finally, crossing the Channel in the version of Mme. Riccoboni, became the rage on the Continent. What was perhaps worse, it completed the transformation of "genteel" into "sentimental" comedy; and, establishing that *genre* for the next few years, effectually retarded the wholesome reac-tion which Goldsmith had sought to promote by the *Good Natur'd Man*.

Meantime that ill-starred work had gone slowly through its last sluggish rehearsals, with a despondent manager, and (for the most part) a desponding cast. Only two of the players were really sympathetic, and these were pretty Mrs. Bulkley, the Miss Richland of the piece, and Shuter, who took the part of Croaker. In the existing state of the public taste, there was considerable doubt about the ex-pediency of playing the bailiff scene in Act III; and when, after much discussion, it was decided to retain it, Colman's last hopes collapsed. Nevertheless, on the 29th of January, six days after the first appearance of Kelly's play, the *Good Natur'd Man* was placed upon the boards at Covent Gar-den. Johnson's prologue, lugubriously delivered by Bensley, the Leontine of the piece, proved depressing rather than exhilarating, while Powell, Garrick's handsome young rival, was stiff and inanimate as the hero, Honeywood. On the other hand Shuter made a hit with Croaker, convulsing the house by his reading of the supposed incendiary letter in Act IV; and Woodward, another admirable comedian, played the impostor Lofty excellently. But, as Colman had predicted, a "genteel" audience could not suffer the bailiffs to come between the wind and its nobility, and after the first representation, Messrs. Twitch and Flanigan were withdrawn. The author, who had attended the first night in his historical suit of Tyrian bloom and satin grain, was bitterly disappointed. Yet although his play ran but for nine nights, three of these brought him profits which reached to £400, to which the sale of the book, with the restored bailiff scene, added some £100 more. Compared with the success of *False Delicacy*, however, these returns were inconsiderable, to say nothing of the fact that sentimentality was not even "scotched." On the contrary, it had assumed a more definite form, and acquired new forces of life.

In all this, the view of posterity must, of necessity, differ from contemporary opinion. Posterity, with its better information, would certainly be disposed to reduce Kelly and exalt Goldsmith. Yet it is by no means certain that, had Kelly's comedy been produced by Colman, and Goldsmith's by Garrick, the position would have been reversed. It is doubtless possible that Garrick's diplomacy could have secured a warmer welcome for the *Good Natur'd Man*, if he had desired that it should succeed. But he could never have created for it the advantages which, in Kelly's case, resulted from an audience attuned to sensibility; and for the nonce, sensibility, whether derived from Richardson or Rousseau, was in the air. *False Delicacy* was mawkish, inadequate, wire-drawn; but it was what its audience wanted. On the other hand, the *Good Natur'd Man*, wholesome and cheery, admirably written, containing as it did, in Croaker and Lofty, two characters which were absolutely new (this was the opinion of that experienced actor Tom Davies), was nevertheless not without some of the drawbacks of a tentative and unpractised stage craft. Garrick was perfectly right in his generation when he doubted the expediency of having in Lofty a personage that occupied a position of almost equal importance with that of Croaker; added to which neither Miss Richland nor Mrs. Croaker contrived to establish any definite hold upon the audience. Nor is it clear that even if Powell had been well or better-disposed to the part, he could have made very much of the weak and amiable Honeywood, while the withdrawal of the bailiff scene must have seriously affected the general gaiety of the whole. Had the *Good Natur'd Man* appeared at a later date, it would have been received with more enthusiasm; but it could never have attained the success of Goldsmith's next effort, *She Stoops to Conquer*.

It was not until five years afterwards that *She Stoops to Conquer* followed its predecessor. For this there were sev-

eral reasons. In the first place, the difficulties of getting the
Good Natur'd Man upon the stage must have been appall-
ing to a needy author; and it was manifest from the success of *False Delicacy* that the comedy of tears must run
its course before the comedy of humour and character
could regain its popularity. Kelly, it is true, did not follow
up his success with equal good fortune. His next piece,
A Word to the Wise (1770), though not inferior to *False
Delicacy*, was a failure. "It was insinuated"—says Hawkins
—"that he was a pensioner of the minister, and, therefore,
a fit object of patriotic vengeance," [5] and after some dis-
orderly proceedings, the play was withdrawn. The sentimental school was, however, recruited by an abler adherent,
Richard Cumberland, whose *West Indian* (1771) repre-
sents the high water-mark in its kind. By this time Goldsmith was recovering his old stage ambition. Whether it
was the success of the *West Indian*, or the failure of *A
Word to the Wise*, which more attracted him, or whether
the success of his poem of the *Deserted Village* had revived
his belief in his own abilities, is difficult to say; but it is
certain that in the autumn of 1771, he was already wander-
ing in the lanes of Hendon and Edgeware "studying jests
with the most tragical countenance" for an as-yet-unnamed
comedy, which was to deserve the success denied to the
Good Natur'd Man. It is to be supposed that it was finished
by the end of 1771.

But finishing it in MS., and getting it acted, were two
different things. Early in 1772 it was apparently in Colman's hands; and in Colman's hands, unhappily, it stayed.
At the end of the year the author was still ignorant what
the manager was going to do; and Goldsmith's repeated
applications for the decision of the enlightened potentate
to whose protection he had fondly hoped (in the Preface
to the *Good Natur'd Man*) "merit would ever be a sufficient passport" remained without definite reply. Meantime
the season, as before, was wasting away, and his needs were
growing urgent. At last, after nearly a year's delay, he
wrote pressingly to Colman. He entreated to be relieved
from his intolerable suspense. Arbitration he would not
endure. But he offered humbly to endeavour to meet all
possible objections, and "not argue about them." He referred frankly to his money difficulties, and begged Colman to take his play, and "let us make the best of it." "Let

[5] *Life of Samuel Johnson, LL.D.*, 1787, p. 518.

me have the same measure at least which you have given
as bad plays as mine." To this moving appeal, which, it is
important to remember, was made on behalf of a comedy
that to this hour keeps the stage, and keeps it worthily,
Colman replied by returning the manuscript, reiterating
his intention to bring out the piece, but freely decorating
the "copy" with vexatious remarks and criticisms. Deeply
mortified, Goldsmith, with no great hope, sent it on as it
was to Garrick. But his kind old Mentor, Johnson, now
intervened. He pointed out the unwisdom of the course
taken, with the result that the play was again hastily withdrawn from Garrick's hands; and Johnson himself went
to see Colman, from whom, by much solicitation, and
even, as the Doctor afterwards described it, the exercise
of "a kind of force," a promise was extracted that the
play should be produced. But even then, it seems, he could
not be persuaded to believe in it. "Dr. Goldsmith," wrote
Johnson a little later,[6] "has a new comedy in rehearsal at
Covent Garden, to which the manager predicts ill-success.
I hope he will be mistaken. I think it deserves a very kind
reception." In another letter to Boswell (24 February
1773) he was more explicit. "Dr. Goldsmith has a new
comedy, which is expected in the spring. No name is yet
given it. The chief diversion arises from a stratagem by
which a lover is made to mistake his future father-in-law's
house for an inn. This, you see, borders upon farce. The
dialogue is quick and gay, and the incidents are so prepared as not to seem improbable."

The "kind reception" which Johnson hoped for his
friend's new effort was, to some extent, promoted by the
appearance of a fresh opponent of sensibility. In February,
1773, a few days before Johnson's last quoted letter, Samuel Foote had produced, at the little theatre in the Haymarket, an entertainment called a *Primitive Puppet Show*,
based upon the Italian Fantoccini, and presenting a bur-
lesque sentimental Comedy called *The Handsome House-
maid; or, Piety in Patterns*, a piece in which—as Foote assured his audience—they would not discover "much wit or
humour," since "his brother writers had all agreed that it
was highly improper, and beneath the dignity of a mixed
assembly, to show any signs of joyful satisfaction; and
that creating a laugh was forcing the higher order of an
audience to a vulgar and mean use of their muscles"—for

[6] To Dr. White, Bishop of Pennsylvania, 4 March, 1773.

which reason, he explained, he had, like them, given up the sensual for the sentimental style. And thereupon followed the story of a maid of low degree who, "by the mere effects of morality and virtue, raised herself [like Richardson's Pamela] to riches and honours." The public, who for some time had acquiesced in the new order of things under the belief that it tended to the reformation of the stage, and who were beginning to weary of the "moral essay thrown into dialogue" which had for some time supplanted humorous situation, promptly came round under the influence of Foote's irresistible Aristophanic ridicule; and the *comédie larmoyante* received an appreciable check. A few weeks earlier Goldsmith himself had endeavoured to aid in the same direction by an essay in the *Westminster Magazine*, from which quotation has already been made.

But notwithstanding these favourable signs of an approaching change in the public taste, the rehearsals of *She Stoops to Conquer* still went on languidly and without great enthusiasm. The Manager's lack of cordiality communicated itself to the company. One after another, the leading actors threw up their parts. That of the first gentleman fell to Lee Lewes, the harlequin of the theatre, while another prominent character had to be entrusted to Quick, who, in the *Good Natur'd Man*, had only filled the subordinate part of a post boy. Garrick, who had adroitly veered with veering public opinion, furnished a prologue in which Sentimental Comedy was stigmatised as a "mawkish drab of spurious breed"; but there were endless troubles about the epilogue, of which no fewer than four versions were composed to meet objections raised by the manager and actresses. What was worse, until a short time before the representation, the play was without a name. Reynolds had suggested *The Belle's Strategem*, a title afterwards adopted by Mrs. Cowley; and another friend, *The Old House, a New Inn*, which had certainly one requisite of a title, the summarising of the story already described by Johnson; while a third proposal was *The Mistakes of a Night*. Finally, recalling a line from Dryden—"But kneels to conquer, and yet stoops to rise"—Goldsmith decided for *She Stoops to Conquer*, to which *The Mistakes of a Night* was added as a sub-title. Then, at length, upon the 15th March, 1773, the play was played; and a few days later published in book form by Francis Newbery, at the

Corner of St. Paul's Churchyard. Goldsmith—says Mr.
Forster—had, up to the last, been so doubtful of success,
that he had hesitated to offer the publisher the copyright
in redemption of a debt between them. But Newbery was
sagacious enough to accept the proposal, "by which he
afterwards very largely profited." The little eighteenpenny
book was inscribed to Johnson with one of those brief
dedications in which "Doctor Minor" is unrivalled. He did
not mean—he said—to compliment his rugged old friend
so much as himself. "It may do me some honour"—he went
on—"to inform the public that I have lived many years in
intimacy with you. It may serve the interests of mankind
also to inform them, that the greatest wit may be found
in a character, without impairing the most unaffected
piety."

Although, as the dedication admits, "the undertaking
of a comedy, not merely sentimental" had been regarded
as "very dangerous," and although Colman had meanly
gone so far as to announce its expected failure in the box
office, *She Stoops to Conquer* was well received. The author's friends, after dining together at a tavern, had gone
down to Covent Garden, headed by Johnson, resolved to
do their best to support the play. But there was no need.
Even Horace Walpole, who had sneered at the "lowness"
of the theme, was constrained to admit that it had "succeeded prodigiously." "All eyes"—says Cumberland—
"were upon Johnson, who sate in a front row of a side
box, and when he laughed every body thought themselves
warranted to roar." Meanwhile Goldsmith was discon-
solately perambulating the Mall. We may borrow what
followed from Mr. Forster. Upon the earnest representation of a friend who found him there, that his presence
might be required at the theatre in case of any sudden
alteration being needed, "he was prevailed upon to go to
the theatre. He entered the stage door at the opening of
the fifth act, and heard a solitary hiss at the improbability
of Mrs. Hardcastle, in her own garden, supposing herself
forty miles off on Crackskull Common (a trick, nevertheless, which Sheridan actually played off on Mme. de
Genlis). 'What's that?' he cried out, alarmed not a little at
the sound. 'Psha! Doctor!' said Colman, who was standing
at the side scene, doubtless well pleased to have even so
much sanction for all his original forebodings: 'don't be
afraid of a squib, when we have been sitting these two

hours on a barrel of gunpowder.' Cooke, who gives the best version of the anecdote,[7] corrects assertions elsewhere made that it had happened at the last rehearsal; tells us that Goldsmith himself had related it to him; and adds that 'he never forgave it to Colman to the last hour of his life.' " The resentment, however, was of brief duration, for Goldsmith died in March of the following year.

With the success of *She Stoops to Conquer*, sentimental comedy may be said to have received a deadly if not fatal blow, and the prolongation of that success, even to our own day, has made censure as idle as it is ungrateful. The accusation of vulgarity, raised by the rose-water critics of its own day, has been negatived by the practice of a long series of students of humour and life, who have asserted and re-asserted its writer's claim to "stoop among the low to copy nature"; while the improbability or farcical character of two of the incidents—the trick played upon Mrs. Hardcastle, and the mistaking of a gentleman's house for an inn—is sufficiently disposed of, for controversial purposes, by the argument that both these things had actually happened. One anomaly has not, we believe, been often mentioned, and that is, that Tony Lumpkin, who in Act IV is so illiterate as not to be able to read more than his own name in script, is clever enough, in Act I, to have composed the excellent song of *The Three Pigeons*. But even thus, in *Twelfth Night*, does Sir Andrew Aguecheek ask the meaning of the word "pourquoi," though we have the assurance of Sir Toby Belch that he is "a scholar" who, in addition to all the good gifts of nature, has "three or four languages word for word without book." Goldsmith's hero, too, has many of the good gifts of nature, and minor blemishes of this sort detract but little from the literary or (what is still more important) the acting quality of the piece, which, for a century and a quarter, has carried out the author's avowed intention of producing laughter. Compared with the *Good Natur'd Man* it was a great advance. Tony Lumpkin and Mr. Hardcastle are better characters than Croaker and Lofty, while the remaining personages, Mrs. Hardcastle, Hastings, young Marlowe, Miss Hardcastle, and Miss Neville, are far beyond the Honeywoods and Richlands of the earlier comedy.

To come to the more material results of the performance. By the three benefit nights Goldsmith must have gained between four and five hundred pounds. Of the twelve nights for which the play was acted at Covent Garden, the tenth was by Royal Command. Foote played it in the summer at the Haymarket; and it was resumed in the winter at Covent Garden, when it was again commanded by royalty; "ran many merry nights that second season; has made thousands of honest people merry, every season since; and still continues to add its yearly sum to the harmless stock of public pleasure." These last lines were written by Mr. Forster in 1848, and they are equally true in 1903. Only a short time ago, Goldsmith's comedy was produced at a London theatre with unabated enthusiasm; and, if the movement which it made in its own time towards the revival of the older and better way of the boards cannot absolutely be said to have been maintained by a series of similar masterpieces, at least it did a great deal to recall the literature of the stage to its best function —that of affording innocent amusement.

AUSTIN DOBSON

Oliver Goldsmith

THE GOOD NATUR'D MAN

On the five octavo editions of *The Good Natur'd Man* printed in 1768, the first, a probable second and third, and the fifth have been accessible in the preparation of this text. In the editions seen, the number is stated only on the title-page of the fifth; and no full collation of all five editions has ever been made. The differences, however, between the missing octavo and the octavos seen are probably very slight, for this volume shows that the differences between even the first and the fifth editions are few. In this text, for the first time, the spelling of the octavos is reproduced, though the capitalization and punctuation, the latter full of vagaries, have been modernized. Goldsmith's frequent treatment of clauses as sentences has been maintained, for it is so consistent as to be a characteristic of his style. On the other hand, the word (*Aside*) after a speech instead of before it has often been changed, for in some instances it was confusing or came too late to be of real use. The collation of the four editions has restored some interesting readings, and has cleared the play of some curious and unwarranted additions. All differences among the editions other than obvious misprints, such as *Merchant Taylor's Hall for Taylors'*, or mere variations in spelling, are given as variants. Corrected readings are from the edition next to the one last named as different. All additions to the text have been placed in brackets. The copies used in the collating have been a first edition from the library of Mr. Robert Hoe, of New York, a probable second in the Boston Public Library, a probable third in the Library of Yale University, and a fifth in the British Museum.

There are two forms of O1. The second has Epi as catchword on p. 74 and gives the epilogue two pages instead of one. The octavo called "a probable second," published like the first and the fifth by W. Griffin, bears just below the author's name, "A New Edition." Except, however, in the correction of the most striking errors of O1, such as *Le Bronze* for *Lofty*; *Waller Congrave* for *Waller; dsepise*, etc., it differs little from O1, preserving most of the errors of O1 corrected in O5. The last line of the epilogue, the same as in O1, and the parenthetical *two very fine things* of Lofty's speech on p. 66 (l. 382), show the closer relation of this octavo to O1 than to O5. It will be called O2. The "probable third" edition has the title-page of O2, but corrects the text more, and in the last line of the epilogue reads like O5.

G. P. B.

PREFACE

When I undertook to write a comedy, I confess I was strongly prepossessed in favour of the poets of the last age, and strove to imitate them. The term, *genteel comedy*,[1] was then unknown amongst us, and little more was desired by an audience than nature and humour in whatever walks of life they were most conspicuous. The author of the following scenes never imagined that more would be expected of him, and therefore to delineate character has been his principal aim. Those who know any thing of composition are sensible that, in pursuing humour, it will sometimes lead us into the recesses of the mean; I was even tempted to look for it in the master of a spunging-house; but in deference to the public taste, grown of late, perhaps, too delicate, the scene of the bailiffs was retrenched in the representation.[2] In deference also to the judgment of a few friends, who think in a particular way, the scene is here restored. The author submits it to the reader in his closet; and hopes that too much refinement will not banish humour and character from our's, as it has already done from the French theatre. Indeed the French comedy[3] is now become so very elevated and sentimental that it has not only banished humour and *Molière* from the stage, but it has banished all spectators too.

Upon the whole, the author returns his thanks to the public for the favourable reception which the *Good Natur'd Man*[4] has met with: and to Mr. Colman in particular, for his kindness[5] to it. It may not also be improper to assure any, who shall hereafter write for the theatre, that merit, or supposed merit, will ever be a sufficient passport to his protection.

[1] See Introduction, pp. 13, 14.
[2] See Act III. pp. 58-64. It was restored to the stage in 1773.
[3] See Introduction, p. 13.
[4] A certain Mr. S——— with this nickname, who figures in Goldsmith's *Life of Richard Nash, of Bath, Esq.*, 1762, p. 85, and who eventually died in gaol, is thought to have suggested this title.
[5] Colman (cf. Introduction) had not been particularly kind to the play. This was the gratitude of success.

PROLOGUE

WRITTEN BY DR. JOHNSON

SPOKEN BY MR. BENSLEY[6]

Prest by the load of life, the weary mind
Surveys the general toil of human kind;
With cool submission joins the labouring train,
And social sorrow loses half it's pain:
Our anxious Bard,[7] without complaint, may share
This bustling season's epidemic care.
Like Cæsar's pilot, dignifi'd by fate,
Tost in one common storm with all the great;
Distrest alike, the statesman and the wit,
When one a borough courts, and one the pit.
The busy candidates for power and fame,
Have hopes, and fears, and wishes, just the same;
Disabled both to combat, or to fly,
Must bear all taunts, and bear without reply.
Uncheck'd [8] on both, loud rabbles vent their rage,
As mongrels bay the lion in a cage.
Th' offended burgess hoards his angry tale,
For that blest year when all that vote may rail;
Their schemes of spite the poet's foes dismiss,
Till that glad night when all that hate may hiss.
This day the powder'd curls and golden coat,

[6] Robert Bensley, 1738-1817, took the part of Leontine in the play. Lamb praises him in his essay "On Some of the Old Actors." He was an excellent Malvolio.

[7] In the Prologue as printed in the *Public Advertiser*, 3 February, 1768, this read: "Our *little* Bard"; but the epithet was altered in deference to the susceptivities of the author. At the same time, two lines which preceded it were withdrawn:—

> "Amidst the toils of this returning year,
>   When senators and nobles learn to fear
>   Our," etc.

[8] The first version reads:—

> "Uncheck'd, on both caprice may vent its rage,
>   As children fret the lion in a cage."

Says swelling Crispin,[9] *begg'd a cobbler's vote.*
This night, our wit, the pert apprentice cries,
Lies at my feet; I hiss him, and he dies.[10]
The great, 'tis true, can charm th' electing tribe;
The bard may supplicate, but cannot bribe.
Yet judg'd by those, whose voices ne'er were sold,
He feels no want of ill persuading gold;
But, confident of praise, if praise be due,
Trusts, without fear, to merit,[11] *and to you.*

[9] A cobbler or shoemaker, of whom St. Crispin was the patron saint. Cf. Shakespeare's *Henry V.* Act iv. Sc. 3.

[10] *This day . . . he dies.* These four lines are not in the first version.

[11] *Merit,* first version, candour.

DRAMATIS PERSONÆ

MEN

Mr. Honeywood

Croaker

Lofty

Sir William Honeywood

Leontine

Jarvis

Butler

Bailiff

Dubardieu

Postboy

WOMEN

Miss Richland

Olivia

Mrs. Croaker

Garnet

Landlady

Scene—London

THE GOOD NATUR'D MAN

ACT THE FIRST

SCENE—*An Apartment in Young* HONEYWOOD's *House*

Enter SIR WILLIAM HONEYWOOD, JARVIS.

SIR WILLIAM. Good Jarvis, make no apologies for this honest bluntness. Fidelity like yours is the best excuse for every freedom.

Jarvis. I can't help being blunt, and being very angry, too, when I hear you talk of disinheriting so good, so worthy a young gentleman as your nephew, my master. All the world loves him.

Sir William. Say rather, that he loves all the world; that is his fault.

Jarvis. I'm sure there is no part of it more dear to him than you are, tho' he has not seen you since he was a child.

Sir William. What signifies his affection to me, or how can I be proud of a place in a heart where every sharper and coxcomb find an easy entrance?

Jarvis. I grant you that he's rather too good natur'd; that he's too much every man's man; that he laughs this minute with one, and cries the next with another; but whose instructions may he thank for all this?

Sir William. Not mine, sure? My letters to him during my employment in Italy taught him only that philosophy which might prevent, not defend his errors.

Jarvis. Faith, begging your honour's pardon, I'm sorry they taught him any philosophy at all; it has only serv'd to spoil him. This same philosophy is a good horse in the stable, but an errant jade on a journey. For my own part, whenever I hear him mention the name on't, I'm always sure he's going to play the fool.

Sir William. Don't let us ascribe his faults to his philosophy, I entreat you. No, Jarvis, his good nature arises rather from his fears of offending the importunate, than his desire of making the deserving happy.

Jarvis. What it rises from, I don't know. But, to be sure, everybody has it that asks it.

Sir William. Ay, or that does not ask it. I have been

now for some time a concealed spectator of his follies, and find them as boundless as his dissipation.

Jarvis. And yet, faith, he has some fine name or other for them all. He calls his extravagance, generosity; and his trusting everybody, universal benevolence. It was but last week he went security for a fellow whose face he scarce knew, and that he call'd an act of exalted mu-mu-munificence; ay, that was the name he gave it.

Sir William. And upon that I proceed, as my last effort, tho' with very little hopes to reclaim him. That very fellow has just absconded, and I have taken up the security. Now, my intention is to involve him in fictitious distress, before he has plunged himself into real calamity. To arrest him for that very debt, to clap an officer upon him, and then let him see which of his friends will come to his relief.

Jarvis. Well, if I could but any way see him thoroughly vexed, every groan of his would be music to me; yet, faith, I believe it impossible. I have tried to fret him myself every morning these three years; but, instead of being angry, he sits as calmly to hear me scold, as he does to his hair-dresser.

Sir William. We must try him once more, however, and I'll go this instant to put my scheme into execution; and I don't despair of succeeding, as, by your means, I can have frequent opportunities of being about him, without being known. What a pity it is, Jarvis, that any man's good will to others should produce so much neglect of himself as to require correction. Yet, we must touch his weaknesses with a delicate hand. There are some faults so nearly allied to excellence, that we can scarce weed out the vice without eradicating the virtue.   [*Exit.*

Jarvis. Well, go thy ways, Sir William Honeywood. It is not without reason that the world allows thee to be the best of men. But here comes his hopeful nephew; the strange good-natur'd, foolish, open-hearted—And yet, all his faults are such that one loves him still the better for them.

Enter HONEYWOOD.

Honeywood. Well, Jarvis, what messages from my friends this morning?

Jarvis. You have no friends.

Honeywood. Well; from my acquaintance then?

Jarvis [*Pulling out bills*]. A few of our usual cards of compliment, that's all. This bill from your taylor; this from your mercer; and this from the little broker in Crooked-lane.[12] He says he has been at a great deal of trouble to get back the money you borrowed.

Honeywood. That I don't know; but I'm sure we were at a great deal of trouble in getting him to lend it.

Jarvis. He has lost all patience.

Honeywood. Then he has lost a very good thing.

Jarvis. There's that ten guineas you were sending to the poor gentleman and his children in the Fleet. I believe that would stop his mouth, for a while at least.

Honeywood. Ay, Jarvis, but what will fill their mouths in the mean time? Must I be cruel because he happens to be importunate; and, to relieve his avarice, leave them to insupportable distress?

Jarvis. 'Sdeath! Sir, the question now is how to relieve yourself. Yourself—Havn't I reason to be out of my senses, when I see things going at sixes and sevens?

Honeywood. Whatever reason you may have for being out of your senses, I hope you'll allow that I'm not quite unreasonable for continuing in mine.

Jarvis. You're the only man alive in your present situation that could do so—Every thing upon the waste. There's Miss Richland and her fine fortune gone already, and upon the point of being given to your rival.

Honeywood. I'm no man's rival.

Jarvis. Your uncle in Italy preparing to disinherit you; your own fortune almost spent; and nothing but pressing creditors, false friends, and a pack of drunken servants that your kindness has made unfit for any other family.

Honeywood. Then they have the more occasion for being in mine.

Jarvis. Soh! What will you have done with him that I caught stealing your plate in the pantry? In the fact; I caught him in the fact.

Honeywood. In the fact! If so, I really think that we should pay him his wages, and turn him off.

Jarvis. He shall be turn'd off at Tyburn, the dog; we'll hang him, if it be only to frighten the rest of the family.

---

[12] There is a Crooked Lane which turns out of Cannon Street, London, though Goldsmith need not have been thinking of it. He also mentions Crooked Lane in Letter LXVIII. of the *Citizen of the World*, 1762, and in Act II. of *She Stoops to Conquer*.

Honeywood. No, Jarvis: it's enough that we have lost what he has stolen; let us not add to it the loss of a fellow creature!

Jarvis. Very fine: well, here was the footman just now, to complain of the butler; he says he does most work, and ought to have most wages.

Honeywood. That's but just; tho' perhaps here comes the butler to complain of the footman.

Jarvis. Ay, it's the way with them all, from the scullion to the privy-counsellor. If they have a bad master, they keep quarrelling with him; if they have a good master, they keep quarrelling with one another.

Enter BUTLER, *drunk*.

Butler. Sir, I'll not stay in the family with Jonathan; you must part with him, or part with me, that's the ex-ex-exposition of the matter, sir.

Honeywood. Full and explicit enough. But what's his fault, good Philip?

Butler. Sir, he's given to drinking, sir, and I shall have my morals corrupted, by keeping such company.

Honeywood. Ha! Ha! He has such a diverting way—

Jarvis. O, quite amusing!

Butler. I find my wines a-going, sir; and liquors don't go without mouths, sir; I hate a drunkard, sir!

Honeywood. Well, well, Philip, I'll hear you upon that another time, so go to bed now.

Jarvis. To bed! Let him go to the devil!

Butler. Begging your honour's pardon, and begging your pardon, Master Jarvis, I'll not go to bed, nor to the devil neither. I have enough to do to mind my cellar. I forgot, your honour, Mr. Croaker is below. I came on purpose to tell you.

Honeywood. Why didn't you shew him up, blockhead?

Butler. Shew him up, sir? With all my heart, sir. Up or down, all's one to me.   [*Exit*.

Jarvis. Ay, we have one or other of that family in this house from morning till night. He comes on the old affair, I suppose. The match between his son, that's just returned from Paris, and Miss Richland, the young lady he's guardian to.

Honeywood. Perhaps so. Mr. Croaker, knowing my friendship for the young lady, has got it into his head that I can persuade her to what I please.

Jarvis. Ah! If you lov'd yourself but half as well as she loves you, we should soon see a marriage that would set all things to rights again.

Honeywood. Love me! Sure, Jarvis, you dream. No, no; her intimacy with me never amounted to more than friendship—mere friendship. That she is the most lovely woman that ever warm'd the human heart with desire, I own. But never let me harbour a thought of making her unhappy by a connection with one so unworthy her merits as I am. No, Jarvis, it shall be my study to serve her, even in spite of my wishes; and to secure her happiness, tho' it destroys my own.

Jarvis. Was ever the like! I want patience.

Honeywood. Besides, Jarvis, tho' I could obtain Miss Richland's consent, do you think I could succeed with her guardian, or Mrs. Croaker, his wife; who, tho' both very fine in their way, are yet a little opposite in their dispositions, you know.

Jarvis. Opposite enough, Heaven knows; the very reverse of each other; she all laugh and no joke; he always complaining and never sorrowful; a fretful, poor soul that has a new distress for every hour in the four and twenty—

Honeywood. Hush, hush, he's coming up, he'll hear you.

Jarvis. One whose voice is a passing bell [13]—

Honeywood. Well, well, go, do.

Jarvis. A raven that bodes nothing but mischief; a coffin and cross bones; a bundle of rue; a sprig of deadly nightshade; a—[HONEYWOOD, *stopping his mouth at last, pushes him off. Exit* JARVIS.

Honeywood. I must own my old monitor is not entirely wrong. There is something in my friend Croaker's conversation that quite depresses me. His very mirth is an antidote to all gaiety, and his appearance has a stronger effect on my spirits than an undertaker's shop.—Mr. Croaker, this is such a satisfaction—

---

[13] The bell that tolls for the dying or dead.

"Before the Passing Bell begun
    The News thro' half the Town has run."
        —Swift's *Verses on his Own Death*, 1739.

Enter CROAKER.[14]

Croaker. A pleasant morning to Mr. Honeywood, and many of them. How is this! You look most shockingly today, my dear friend. I hope this weather does not affect your spirits. To be sure, if this weather continues—I say nothing—But God send we be all better this day three months.

Honeywood. I heartily concur in the wish, tho', I own, not in your apprehensions.

Croaker. May be not! Indeed what signifies what weather we have in a country going to ruin like ours? Taxes rising and trade falling. Money flying out of the kingdom and Jesuits swarming into it. I know at this time no less than an hundred and twenty-seven Jesuits between Charing-cross and Temple-bar.

Honeywood. The Jesuits will scarce pervert you or me, I should hope.

Croaker. May be not. Indeed what signifies whom they pervert in a country that has scarce any religion to lose? I'm only afraid for our wives and daughters.

Honeywood. I have no apprehensions for the ladies, I assure you.

Croaker. May be not. Indeed what signifies whether they be perverted or no? The women in my time were good for something. I have seen a lady dressed from top to toe in her own manufactures formerly. But now-a-days, the devil a thing of their own manufactures about them, except their faces.

Honeywood. But, however these faults may be practised abroad, you don't find them at home, either with Mrs. Croaker, Olivia or Miss Richland.

Croaker. The best of them will never be canoniz'd for a saint when she's dead. By the bye, my dear friend, I don't find this match between Miss Richland and my son much relish'd, either by one side or t'other.

Honeywood. I thought otherwise.

Croaker. Ah, Mr. Honeywood, a little of your fine serious advice to the young lady might go far: I know she has a very exalted opinion of your understanding.

[14] This character is affirmed to have been based on the "Suspirius" of Dr. Johnson (*Rambler*, 1750, No. 59). But there is a votary of borrowed misery in Letters LXXXIX. of Goldsmith's own *Citizen of the World*, 1762.

Honeywood. But would not that be usurping an authority that more properly belongs to yourself?

Croaker. My dear friend, you know but little of my authority at home. People think, indeed, because they see me come out in a morning thus, with a pleasant face, and to make my friends merry, that all's well within. But I have cares that would break an heart of stone. My wife has so encroach'd upon every one of my privileges, that I'm now no more than a mere lodger in my own house!

Honeywood. But a little spirit exerted on your side might perhaps restore your authority.

Croaker. No, tho' I had the spirit of a lion! I do rouze sometimes. But what then! Always hagling and hagling. A man is tired of getting the better before his wife is tired of losing the victory.

Honeywood. It's a melancholy consideration indeed, that our chief comforts often produce our greatest anxieties, and that an encrease of our possessions is but an inlet to new disquietudes.

Croaker. Ah, my dear friend, these were the very words of poor Dick Doleful to me not a week before he made away with himself. Indeed, Mr. Honeywood, I never see you but you put me in mind of poor—Dick. Ah, there was merit neglected for you! and so true a friend; we lov'd each other for thirty years, and yet he never asked me to lend him a single farthing!

Honeywood. Pray what could induce him to commit so rash an action at last?

Croaker. I don't know. Some people were malicious enough to say it was keeping company with me; because we us'd to meet now and then and open our hearts to each other. To be sure, I lov'd to hear him talk, and he lov'd to hear me talk; poor dear Dick. He used to say that Croaker rhim'd to joker; and so we used to laugh— Poor Dick.   [*Going to cry.*

Honeywood. His fate affects me.

Croaker. Ay, he grew sick of this miserable life, where we do nothing but eat and grow hungry, dress and undress, get up and lie down; while reason, that should watch like a nurse by our side, falls as fast asleep as we do.

Honeywood. To say truth,[15] if we compare that part of

[15] This seems to be a memory of the second paragraph of Letter LXX. in the *Citizen of the World*, 1762:—"If I should judge of that part of life which lies before me by that which I have already seen, the prospect is hideous."

life which is to come by that which we have past, the prospect is hideous.

Croaker. Life at the greatest and best is but a froward child, that must be humour'd and coax'd a little till it falls asleep, and then all the care is over.[16]

Honeywood. Very true, sir, nothing can exceed the vanity of our existence but the folly of our pursuits. We wept when we came into the world, and every day tells us why.

Croaker. Ah, my dear friend, it is a perfect satisfaction to be miserable with you. My son Leontine shan't lose the benefit of such fine conversation. I'll just step home for him. I am willing to shew him so much seriousness in one scarce older than himself—And what if I bring my last letter to the *Gazetteer* on the encrease and progress of earthquakes? It will amuse us, I promise you. I there prove how the late earthquake[17] is coming round to pay us another visit from London to Lisbon, from Lisbon to the Canary Islands, from the Canary Islands to Palmyra, from Palmyra to Constantinople, and so from Constantinople back to London again.   [*Exit.*

Honeywood. Poor Croaker! His situation deserves the utmost pity. I shall scarce recover my spirits these three days. Sure, to live upon such terms is worse than death itself. And yet, when I consider my own situation—a broken fortune, an hopeless passion, friends in distress, the wish but not the power to serve them—[*Pausing and sighing.*

Enter BUTLER.

Butler. More company below, sir; Mrs. Croaker and Miss Richland; shall I shew them up? But they're shewing up themselves.   [*Exit.*

Enter MRS. CROAKER *and* MISS RICHLAND.

Miss Richland. You're always in such spirits.

Mrs. Croaker. We have just come, my dear Honeywood, from the auction.[18] There was the old deaf dowager, as

[16] This is an unconscious recollection of a rhythmical passage at the end of Sir William Temple's essay on Poetry (*Works*, 1720, i, p. 249). Lamb quotes it in closing his essay on "The Genteel Style in Writing" (Shaftesbury and Temple).

[17] There had been an earthquake at Martinique, August, 1767.

[18] The eighteenth-century auction-room was a favourite re-

usual, bidding like a fury against herself. And then so curious in antiques! [19] Herself the most genuine piece of antiquity in the whole collection!

Honeywood. Excuse me, ladies, if some uneasiness from friendship makes me unfit to share in this good humour: I know you'll pardon me.

Mrs. Croaker. I vow he seems as melancholy as if he had taken a dose of my husband this morning. Well, if Richland here can pardon you, I must.

Miss Richland. You would seem to insinuate, madam, that I have particular reasons for being dispos'd to refuse it.

Mrs. Croaker. Whatever I insinuate, my dear, don't be so ready to wish an explanation.

Miss Richland. I own I should be sorry Mr. Honeywood's long friendship and mine should be misunderstood.

Honeywood. There's no answering for others, madam. But I hope you'll never find me presuming to offer more than the most delicate friendship may readily allow.

Miss Richland. And I shall be prouder of such a tribute from you than the most passionate professions from others.

Honeywood. My own sentiments, madam: friendship is a disinterested commerce between equals; love, an abject intercourse between tyrants and slaves.

Miss Richland. And, without a compliment, I know none more disinterested or more capable of friendship than Mr. Honeywood.

Mrs. Croaker. And indeed I know nobody that has more friends, at least among the ladies. Miss Fruzz, Miss Odbody and Miss Winterbottom, praise him in all companies. As for Miss Biddy Bundle, she's his professed admirer.

Miss Richland. Indeed! an admirer! I did not know, sir, you were such a favourite there. But is she seriously so handsome? Is she the mighty thing talk'd of?

Honeywood. The town, madam, seldom begins to praise a lady's beauty till she's beginning to lose it! (*Smiling.*)

Mrs. Croaker. But she's resolved never to lose it, it seems. For as her natural face decays, her skill improves in making the artificial one. Well, nothing diverts me more than one of those fine old dressy things, who thinks

sort of persons of quality. A famous one was that of Cock (Fielding's "Mr. Auctioneer Hen") in the Great Piazza, Covent Garden.

[19] *Curious in antiques,* an amateur of antiques, curiosities.

to conceal her age by every where exposing her person; sticking herself up in the front of a side-box;[20] trailing thro' a minuet at Almack's; and then, in the public gardens; looking for all the world like one of the painted ruins[21] of the place.

Honeywood. Every age has its admirers, ladies. While you, perhaps, are trading among the warmer climates of youth, there ought to be some to carry on an useful commerce in the frozen latitudes beyond fifty.

Miss Richland. But then the mortifications they must suffer before they can be fitted out for traffic. I have seen one of them fret an whole morning at her hair-dresser, when all the fault was on her face.

Honeywood. And yet I'll engage has carried that face at last to a very good market. This good-natur'd town, madam, has husbands, like spectacles, to fit every age, from fifteen to fourscore.

Mrs. Croaker. Well, you're a dear good-natur'd creature. But you know you're engaged with us this morning upon a strolling party. I want to shew Olivia the town, and the things; I believe I shall have business for you for the whole day.

Honeywood. I am sorry, madam, I have an appointment with Mr. Croaker which it is impossible to put off.

Mrs. Croaker. What! with my husband! Then I'm resolved to take no refusal. Nay, I protest you must. You know I never laugh so much as with you.

Honeywood. Why, if I must, I must. I'll swear you have put me into such spirits. Well, do you find jest, and I'll find laugh, I promise you. We'll wait for the chariot in the next room.   [*Exeunt.*

Enter LEONTINE *and* OLIVIA.

Leontine. There they go, thoughtless and happy. My dearest Olivia, what would I give to see you capable of sharing in their amusements, and as chearful as they are.

Olivia. How, my Leontine, how can I be chearful, when I have so many terrors to oppress me! The fear of

[20] It was from the front row of a side-box that Johnson and his party witnessed the first representation of *She Stoops to Conquer* (Cumberland's *Memoirs*, 1807, i, p. 368).

[21] These were the painted architectural scenes—ruins of Palmyra and the like—which terminated the chief walks at Old Vauxhall Gardens.

being detected by this family, and the apprehensions of a censuring world when I must be detected—

Leontine. The world!—my love, what can it say? At worst it can only say that, being compelled by a mercenary guardian to embrace a life you disliked, you formed a resolution of flying with the man of your choice; that you confided in his honour, and took refuge in my father's house;[22] the only one where your's could remain without censure.

Olivia. But consider, Leontine, your disobedience and my indiscretion; your being sent to France to bring home a sister, and, instead of a sister, bringing home—

Leontine. One dearer than a thousand sisters. One that I am convinc'd will be equally dear to the rest of the family when she comes to be known.

Olivia. And that, I fear, will shortly be.

Leontine. Impossible, 'till we ourselves think proper to make the discovery. My sister, you know has been with her aunt, at Lyons, since, she was a child, and you find every creature in the family takes you for her.

Olivia. But mayn't she write, mayn't her aunt write?

Leontine. Her aunt scarce ever writes, and all my sister's letters are directed to me.

Olivia. But won't your refusing Miss Richland, for whom you know the old gentleman intends you, create a suspicion?

Leontine. There, there's my master-stroke. I have resolved not to refuse her; nay, an hour hence I have consented to go with my father, to make her an offer of my heart and fortune.

Olivia. Your heart and fortune!

Leontine. Don't be alarm'd, my dearest. Can Olivia think so meanly of my honour, or my love, as to suppose I could ever hope for happiness from any but her? No, my Olivia, neither the force, nor, permit me to add, the delicacy of my passion, leave any room to suspect me. I only offer Miss Richland an heart I am convinc'd she will refuse; as I am confident that, without knowing it, her affections are fixed upon Mr. Honeywood.

Olivia. Mr. Honeywood! You'll excuse my apprehensions; but when your merits come to be put in the ballance—

[22] O1, O2, this house.

Leontine. You view them with too much partiality. However, by making this offer, I shew a seeming compliance with my father's commands; and perhaps, upon her refusal, I may have his consent to chuse for myself.

Olivia. Well, I submit. And yet, my Leontine, I own, I shall envy her even your pretended addresses. I consider every look, every expression of your esteem, as due only to me. This is folly, perhaps: I allow it, but it is natural to suppose that merit which has made an impression on ones own heart may be powerful over that of another.

Leontine. Don't, my life's treasure, don't let us make imaginary evils when you know we have so many real ones to encounter. At worst, you know, if Miss Richland should consent, or my father refuse his pardon, it can but end in a trip to Scotland;[23] and—

Enter CROAKER.

Croaker. Where have you been, boy? I have been seeking you. My friend Honeywood here has been saying such comfortable things. Ah, he's an example indeed! Where is he? I left him here.

Leontine. Sir, I believe you may see him, and hear him, too, in the next room; he's preparing to go out with the ladies.

Croaker. Good gracious, can I believe my eyes or my ears! I'm struck dumb with his vivacity and stunn'd with the loudness of his laugh. Was there ever such a transformation! [*A laugh behind the scenes;* CROAKER *mimics it.*] Ha! ha! ha! there it goes; a plague take their balderdash; yet I could expect nothing less, when my precious wife was of the party. On my conscience, I believe she could spread an horse-laugh thro' the pews of a tabernacle.[24]

Leontine. Since you find so many objections to a wife, sir, how can you be so earnest in recommending one to me?

Croaker. I have told you, and tell you again, boy, that Miss Richland's fortune must not go out of the family; one may find comfort in the money, whatever one does in the wife.

Leontine. But, sir, tho', in obedience to your desire, I

[23] See the essay on "Scotch Marriages."

[24] Goldsmith was probably thinking of Whitefield's Tabernacle in Tottenham Court Road. (See last paragraph of essay on "The Theatre.")

am ready to marry her, it may be possible she has no inclination to me.

Croaker. I'll tell you once for all how it stands. A good part of Miss Richland's large fortune consists in a claim upon Government, which my good friend Mr. Lofty[25] assures me the Treasury will allow. One half of this she is to forfeit, by her father's will, in case she refuses to marry you. So, if she rejects you, we seize half her fortune; if she accepts you, we seize the whole, and a fine girl into the bargain.

Leontine. But, sir, if you will but listen to reason—

Croaker. Come, then, produce your reasons. I tell you I'm fix'd, determined; so now produce your reasons. When I'm determined, I always listen to reason, because it can then do no harm.

Leontine. You have alleged that a mutual choice was the first requisite in matrimonial happiness.

Croaker. Well, and you have both of you a mutual choice. She has her choice—to marry you, or lose half her fortune; and you have your choice—to marry her, or pack out of doors without any fortune at all.

Leontine. An only son, sir, might expect more indulgence.

Croaker. An only father, sir, might expect more obedience; besides, has not your sister here, that never disobliged me in her life, as good a right as you? He's a sad dog, Livy, my dear, and would take all from you. But he shan't, I tell you he shan't, for you shall have your share.

Olivia. Dear sir, I wish you'd be convinced that I can never be happy in any addition to my fortune which is taken from his.

Croaker. Well, well, it's a good child, so say no more, but come with me, and we shall see something that will give us a great deal of pleasure, I promise you: old Ruggins, the curry-comb-maker, lying in state;[26] I'm told he makes a very handsome corpse, and becomes his coffin prodigiously. He was an intimate friend of mine, and these are friendly things we ought to do for each other.

[*Exeunt.*

[25] O1, friend, Mr. Le Bronze.

[26] This was a common practice with all classes in the eighteenth century, to which Goldsmith had devoted a letter (No. xii.) in the *Citizen of the World,* 1762. Montesquieu (*Lettres Persanes,* 1721, xl.) and Voltaire also complained of the contemporary manner of conducting funerals.

ACT THE SECOND

SCENE—CROAKER'S *House*

MISS RICHLAND, GARNET.

MISS RICHLAND. Olivia not his sister? Olivia not Leontine's sister? You amaze me!

Garnet. No more his sister than I am; I had it all from his own servant; I can get any thing from that quarter.

Miss Richland. But how? Tell me again, Garnet.

Garnet. Why, madam, as I told you before, instead of going to Lyons to bring home his sister, who has been there with her aunt these ten years, he never went further than Paris; there he saw and fell in love with this young lady—by the bye, of a prodigious family.[27]

Miss Richland. And brought her home to my guardian, as his daughter?

Garnet. Yes, and daughter she will be; if he don't consent to their marriage, they talk of trying what a Scotch parson can do.

Miss Richland. Well, I own they have deceived me— And so demurely as Olivia carried it, too!—Would you believe it, Garnet, I told her all my secrets; and yet the sly cheat concealed all this from me?

Garnet. And, upon my word, madam, I don't much blame her; she was loath to trust one with her secrets that was so very bad at keeping her own.

Miss Richland. But, to add to their deceit, the young gentleman, it seems, pretends to make me serious proposals. My guardian and he are to be here presently, to open the affair in form. You know I am to lose half my fortune if I refuse him.

Garnet. Yet, what can you do? For being, as you are, in love with Mr. Honeywood, madam—

Miss Richland. How, ideot! what do you mean? In love with Mr. Honeywood! Is this to provoke me?

Garnet. That is, madam, in friendship with him; I meant nothing more than friendship, as I hope to be married; nothing more.

[27] Prodigious here no doubt means very old.

Miss Richland. Well, no more of this! As to my guardian and his son, they shall find me prepared to receive them; I'm resolved to accept their proposal with seeming pleasure, to mortify them by compliance, and so throw the refusal at last upon them.

Garnet. Delicious! and that will secure your whole fortune to yourself. Well, who could have thought so innocent a face could cover so much cuteness!

Miss Richland. Why, girl, I only oppose my prudence to their cunning, and practise a lesson they have taught me against themselves.

Garnet. Then you're likely not long to want employment, for here they come, and in close conference!

Enter CROAKER, LEONTINE.

Leontine. Excuse me, sir, if I seem to hesitate upon the point of putting the lady so important a question.

Croaker. Lord! good sir, moderate your fears; you're so plaguy shy that one would think you had changed sexes. I tell you we must have the half or the whole. Come, let me see with what spirit you begin? Well, why don't you? Eh! What? Well then—I must, it seems—Miss Richland, my dear, I believe you guess at our business—an affair which my son here comes to open, that nearly concerns your happiness.

Miss Richland. Sir, I should be ungrateful not to be pleased with any thing that comes recommended by you.

Croaker. How, boy, could you desire a finer opening? Why don't you begin, I say?   [*To* LEONTINE.

Leontine. 'Tis true, madam, my father, madam, has some intentions—hem—of explaining an affair—which —himself—can best explain, madam.

Croaker. Yes, my dear; it comes intirely from my son; it's all a request of his own, madam. And I will permit him to make the best of it.

Leontine. The whole affair is only this, madam; my father has a proposal to make which he insists none but himself shall deliver.

Croaker [*Aside*]. My mind misgives me, the fellow will never be brought on.—In short, madam, you see before you one that loves you; one whose whole happiness is all in you.

Miss Richland. I never had any doubts of your regard, sir; and I hope you can have none of my duty.

Croaker. That's not the thing, my little sweeting; my love! No, no, another guess lover[28] than I; there he stands, madam; his very looks declare the force of his passion!— Call up a look, you dog—But then, had you seen him, as I have, weeping, speaking soliloquies and blank verse, sometimes melancholy, and sometimes absent—

Miss Richland. I fear, sir, he's absent now; or such a declaration would have come most properly from himself.

Croaker. Himself, madam! he would die before he could make such a confession; and if he had not a channel for his passion thro' me, it would ere now have drowned his understanding.

Miss Richland. I must grant, sir, there are attractions in modest diffidence above the force of words. A silent address is the genuine eloquence of sincerity.

Croaker. Madam, he has forgot to speak any other language; silence is become his mother tongue.

Miss Richland. And it must be confessed, sir, it speaks very powerfully in his favour. And yet, I shall be thought too forward in making such a confession; shan't I, Mr. Leontine?

Leontine [*Aside*]. Confusion! my reserve will undo me. But, if modesty attracts her, impudence may disgust her. I'll try.—Don't imagine from my silence, madam, that I want a due sense of the honour and happiness intended me. My father, madam, tells me your humble servant is not totally indifferent to you. He admires you; I adore you; and when we come together, upon my soul I believe we shall be the happiest couple in all St. James's!

Miss Richland. If I could flatter myself you thought as you speak, sir—

Leontine. Doubt my sincerity, madam? By your dear self I swear! Ask the brave if they desire glory; ask cowards if they covert safety—

Croaker. Well, well, no more questions about it.

Leontine. Ask the sick if they long for health, ask misers if they love money, ask—

Croaker. Ask a fool if he can talk nonsense! What's come over the boy? What signifies asking, when there's not a soul to give you an answer? If you would ask to the purpose, ask this lady's consent to make you happy.

---

[28] An otherguess lover, a lover of another guise, or fashion.

Miss Richland. Why, indeed, sir, his uncommon ardour almost compels me, forces me, to comply. And yet I'm afraid he'll despise a conquest gain'd with too much ease; won't you, Mr. Leontine?

Leontine [*Aside*]. Confusion!—O, by no means, madam, by no means. And yet, madam, you talk'd of force. There is nothing I would avoid so much as compulsion in a thing of this kind. No, madam, I will still be generous, and leave you at liberty to refuse.

Croaker. But I tell you, sir, the lady is not at liberty. Its a match. You see she says nothing. Silence gives consent.

Leontine. But, sir, she talk'd of force. Consider, sir, the cruelty of constraining her inclinations.

Croaker. But I say there's no cruelty. Don't you know, blockhead, that girls have always a roundabout way of saying yes before company? So get you both gone together into the next room, and hang him that interrupts the tender explanation. Get you gone, I say; I'll not hear a word.

Leontine. But, sir, I must beg leave to insist—

Croaker. Get off, you puppy, or I'll beg leave to insist upon knocking you down. Stupid whelp! But I don't wonder, the boy takes entirely after his mother!

[*Exeunt* Miss Richland *and* Leontine.

Enter Mrs. Croaker.

Mrs. Croaker. Mr. Croaker, I bring you something, my dear, that I believe will make you smile.

Croaker. I'll hold you a guinea of that, my dear.

Mrs. Croaker. A letter; and, as I knew the hand, I ventured to open it.

Croaker. And how can you expect your breaking open my letters should give me pleasure?

Mrs. Croaker. Poo, it's from your sister at Lyons, and contains good news: read it.

Croaker. What a Frenchified cover is here! That sister of mine has some good qualities, but I could never teach her to fold a letter.[29]

---

[29] This, before envelopes, was a fine art. Cf. Praed's *Belle of the Ball-Room* (*Poems*, 1864, ii. 148):—

"She wrote a charming hand—and oh!
How sweetly all her notes were folded!"

Mrs. Croaker. Fold a fiddlestick! Read what it contains.
Croaker [*reading*].[30]

Dear Nick,

An English gentleman, of large fortune, has for some time made private, tho' honourable proposals to your daughter Olivia. They love each other tenderly, and I find she has consented, without letting any of the family know, to crown his addresses. As such good offers don't come every day, your own good sense, his large fortune, and family considerations, will induce you to forgive her.

Yours ever,

Rachel Croaker.[31]

My daughter, Olivia, privately contracted to a man of large fortune! This is good news indeed! My heart never foretold me of this. And yet, how slily the little baggage has carried it since she came home. Not a word on't to the old ones for the world! Yet, I thought I saw something she wanted to conceal.

Mrs. Croaker. Well, if they have concealed their amour, they shan't conceal their wedding; that shall be public, I'm resolved.

Croaker. I tell thee, woman, the wedding is the most foolish part of the ceremony. I can never get this woman to think of the more serious part of the nuptial engagement.

Mrs. Croaker. What, would you have me think of their funeral? But come, tell me, my dear, don't you owe more to me than you care to confess? Would you have ever been known to Mr. Lofty, who has undertaken Miss Richland's claim at the Treasury, but for me? Who was it first made him an acquaintance at Lady Shabbaroon's route? Who got him to promise us his interest? Is not he a back-stairs favourite, one that can do what he pleases with those that do what they please? Isn't he an acquaintance that all your groaning and lamentations could never have got us?

Croaker. He is a man of importance, I grant you. And yet, what amazes me is, that while he is giving away places to all the world, he can't get one for himself.

---

[30] *Croaker* [*reading*]. In O1 and O2, this direction is set as text.

[31] O1, O2 set this:—*Yours ever—Rachel Croaker.*

Mrs. Croaker. That perhaps may be owing to his nicety. Great men are not easily satisfied!

Enter FRENCH SERVANT.

Servant. An expresse from Monsieur Lofty. He vil be vait upon your honours instammant.[32] He be only giving four five instruction, read two tree memorial, call upon von ambassadeur! He vil be vid you in one tree minutes.

Mrs. Croaker. You see now, my dear. What an extensive department! [33] Well, friend, let your master know, that we are extremely honoured by this honour. Was there any thing ever in a higher style of breeding! All messages among the great are now done by express.

Croaker. To be sure, no man does little things with more solemnity, or claims more respect than he. But he's in the right on't. In our bad world, respect is given where respect is claimed.

Mrs. Croaker. Never mind the world, my dear; you were never in a pleasanter place in your life. Let us now think of receiving him with proper respect [*a loud rapping at the door*], and there he is, by the thundering rap.

Croaker. Ay, verily, there he is; as close upon the heels of his own express as an indorsement upon the back of a bill. Well, I'll leave you to receive him, whilst I go to chide my little Olivia for intending to steal a marriage without mine or her aunt's consent. I must seem to be angry, or she, too, may begin to despise my authority.

[*Exit.*

Enter LOFTY, *speaking to his* SERVANT.

Lofty. And if the Venetian Ambassador, or that teasing creature the Marquis, should call, I'm not at home. Dam'me, I'll be pack-horse to none of them! My dear madam, I have just snatched a moment—And if the expresses to his Grace be ready, let them be sent off; they're of importance. Madam, I ask a thousand pardons!

Mrs. Croaker. Sir, this honour—

Lofty. And, Dubardieu! If the person calls about the commission, let him know that it is made out. As for Lord Cumbercourt's stale request, it can keep cold: you understand me. Madam, I ask ten thousand pardons!

[32] *Instammant;* from O1-O3. In O5, *instrammant.*
[33] This must mean field of operation, as Lofty was not in office.

Mrs. Croaker. Sir this honour—

Lofty. And, Dubardieu! If the man comes from the Cornish borough, you must do him; you must do him, I say. Madam, I ask ten thousand pardons. And if the Russian-Ambassador calls: but he will scarce call to-day, I believe. And now, madam, I have just got time to express my happiness in having the honour of being permitted to profess myself your most obedient, humble servant!

Mrs. Croaker. Sir, the happiness and honour are all mine; and yet, I'm only robbing the public while I detain you.

Lofty. Sink the public, madam, when the fair are to be attended. Ah, could all my hours be so charmingly devoted![34] Sincerely, don't you pity us poor creatures in affairs? Thus it is eternally; solicited for places here, teized for pensions there, and courted every where. I know you pity me. Yes, I see you do.

Mrs. Croaker. Excuse me, sir. "Toils of empires pleasures are," as Waller says.[35]

Lofty. Waller, Waller; is he of the House?

Mrs. Croaker. The modern poet of that name, sir.

Lofty. Oh, a modern! We men of business despise the moderns; and as for the ancients, we have no time to read them. Poetry is a pretty thing enough for our wives and daughters; but not for us. Why now, here I stand that know nothing of books. I say, madam, I know nothing of books; and yet, I believe, upon a land carriage fishery,[36] a stamp act, or a jag-hire, I can talk my two hours without feeling the want of them.

Mrs. Croaker. The world is no stranger to Mr. Lofty's eminence in every capacity!

Lofty. I vow to Gad, madam, you make me blush. I'm nothing, nothing, nothing in the world; a mere obscure gentleman! To be sure, indeed, one or two of the present ministers are pleased to represent me as a formidable[37] man. I know they are pleased to be-spatter me at all their little dirty levees. Yet, upon my soul, I wonder what they see in me to treat me so! Measures, not men,[38] have always

[34] *Devoted.* O5 corrects devouted.

[35] O1, Waller Congrave says.

[36] Fish machines for carrying fish by land to London were established in 1761.

[37] *Formidable.* O1 and O2, formal.

[38] This seems to have been a current political phrase. Lord Chesterfield uses it in a letter to Dr. Chenevix as early as March, 1742.

been my mark; and I vow, by all that's honourable, my resentment has never done the men, as mere men, any manner of harm—That is, as mere men.

Mrs. Croaker. What importance, and yet what modesty!

Lofty. Oh, if you talk of modesty, madam! There, I own, I'm accessible to praise. Modesty is my foible: it was so the Duke of Brentford used to say of me. "I love Jack Lofty," he used to say: "no man has a finer knowledge of things; quite a man of information; and when he speaks upon his legs, by the lord, he's prodigious, he scouts them; and yet all men have their faults; too much modesty is his," says his Grace.

Mrs. Croaker. And yet, I dare say, you don't want assurance when you come to solicit for your friends.

Lofty. O, there indeed I'm in bronze.[39] Apropos, I have just been mentioning Miss Richland's case to a certain personage; we must name no names. When I ask, I am not to be put off, madam. No, no, I take my friend by the button. A fine girl, sir; great justice in her case. A friend of mine. Borough interest. Business must be done, Mr. Secretary. I say, Mr. Secretary, her business must be done, sir. That's my way, madam!

Mrs. Croaker. Bless me! you said all this to the Secretary of State, did you?

Lofty. I did not say the Secretary, did I? Well, curse it, since you have found me out, I will not deny it. It was to the Secretary.

Mrs. Croaker. This was going to the fountain head at once, not applying to the understrappers, as Mr. Honeywood would have had us.

Lofty. Honeywood! he! he! He was, indeed, a fine solicitor. I suppose you have heard what has just happened to him?

Mrs. Croaker. Poor dear man, no accident, I hope!

Lofty. Undone, madam, that's all. His creditors have taken him into custody. A prisoner in his own house!

Mrs. Croaker. A prisoner in his own house! How! At this very time! I'm quite unhappy for him.

Lofty. Why, so am I! The man, to be sure, was immensely good natur'd. But then, I could never find that he had any thing in him.

Mrs. Croaker. His manner, to be sure, was excessive

---

[39] This is no doubt a forgotten reference to Lofty's first name of Le Bronze.

harmless; some, indeed, thought it a little dull. For my part, I always concealed my opinion.

Lofty. It can't be conceal'd, madam; the man was dull, dull as the last new comedy! [40] A poor impracticable creature! I tried once or twice to know if he was fit for business; but he had scarce talents to be groom-porter to an orange barrow!

Mrs. Croaker. How differently does Miss Richland think of him! For, I believe, with all his faults, she loves him.

Lofty. Loves him! Does she? You should cure her of that, by all means. Let me see: what if she were sent to him this instant, in his present doleful situation? My life for it, that works her cure! Distress is a perfect antidote to love. Suppose we join her in the next room? Miss Richland is a fine girl, has a fine fortune,[41] and must not be thrown away. Upon my honour, madam, I have a regard for Miss Richland; and, rather than she should be thrown away, I should think it no indignity to marry her myself.

[*Exeunt.*

Enter OLIVIA *and* LEONTINE.

Leontine. And yet, trust me, Olivia, I had every reason to expect Miss Richland's refusal, as I did every thing in my power to deserve it. Her indelicacy surprizes me.

Olivia. Sure, Leontine, there's nothing so indelicate in being sensible of your merit. If so, I fear, I shall be the most guilty thing alive.

Leontine. But you mistake, my dear. The same attention I used to advance my merit with you, I practised to lessen it with her. What more could I do?

Olivia. Let us now rather consider what's to be done. We have both dissembled too long—I have always been asham'd—I am now quite weary of it. Sure, I could never have undergone so much for any other but you.

Leontine. And you shall find my gratitude equal to your kindest compliance. Tho' our friends should totally forsake us, Olivia, we can draw upon content for the deficiencies of fortune.

Olivia. Then why should we defer our scheme of humble happiness when it is now in our power? I may be the

[40] This was Kelly's *False Delicacy.* But Goldsmith could scarcely have referred to this here. See Introduction, pp. 16-17.

[41] *Has a fine fortune.* O1 and O2 read, and has; and after *fortune*, within dashes, two very fine things.

favourite of your father, it is true; but can it ever be thought that his present kindness to a suppos'd child will continue to a known deceiver?

Leontine. I have many reasons to believe it will. As his attachments are but few, they are lasting. His own marriage was a private one, as our's may be. Besides, I have sounded him already at a distance, and find all his answers exactly to our wish. Nay, by an expression or two that drop'd from him, I am induced to think he knows of this affair.

Olivia. Indeed! But that would be an happiness too great to be expected.

Leontine. However it be, I'm certain you have power over him; and am persuaded, if you inform'd him of our situation, that he would be disposed to pardon it.

Olivia. You had equal expectations, Leontine, from your last scheme with Miss Richland, which you find has succeeded most wretchedly.

Leontine. And that's the best reason for trying another.

Olivia. If it must be so, I submit.

Leontine. As we could wish, he comes this way. Now, my dearest Olivia, be resolute. I'll just retire within hearing, to come in at a proper time, either to share your danger, or confirm your victory.   [*Exit.*

Enter CROAKER.

Croaker. Yes, I must forgive her; and yet not too easily, neither. It will be proper to keep up the decorums of resentment a little, if it be only to impress her with an idea of my authority.

Olivia. How I tremble to approach him!—Might I presume, sir—If I interrupt you—

Croaker. No, child, where I have an affection, it is not a little thing can interrupt me. Affection gets over little things.

Olivia. Sir, you're too kind! I'm sensible how ill I deserve this partiality. Yet, Heaven knows, there is nothing I would not do to gain it.

Croaker. And you have but too well succeeded, you little hussey, you! With those endearing ways of yours, on my conscience, I could be brought to forgive any thing, unless it were a very great offence indeed.

Olivia. But mine is such an offence—When you know

my guilt—Yes, you shall know it, tho' I feel the greatest pain in the confession.

Croaker. Why, then, if it be so very great a pain, you may spare yourself the trouble, for I know every syllable of the matter before you begin.

Olivia. Indeed! Then I'm undone!

Croaker. Ay, miss, you wanted to steal a match, without letting me know it, did you! But I'm not worth being consulted, I suppose, when there's to be a marriage in my own family! No, I'm to have no hand in the disposal of my own children! No, I'm nobody! I'm to be a mere article of family lumber; a piece of crack'd china to be stuck up in a corner!

Olivia. Dear sir, nothing but the dread of your authority could induce us to conceal it from you.

Croaker. No, no, my consequence is no more; I'm as little minded as a dead Russian in winter, just stuck up with a pipe in his mouth till there comes a thaw—It goes to my heart to vex her.

Olivia. I was prepar'd, sir, for your anger, and despair'd of pardon, even while I presum'd to ask it. But your severity shall never abate my affection, as my punishment is but justice.

Croaker. And yet you should not despair neither, Livy. We ought to hope all for the best.

Olivia. And do you permit me to hope, sir! Can I ever expect to be forgiven? But hope has too long deceiv'd me!

Croaker. Why then, child, it shan't deceive you now, for I forgive you this very moment. I forgive you all; and now you are indeed my daughter.

Olivia. O transport! This kindness overpowers me!

Croaker. I was always against severity to our children. We have been young and giddy ourselves, and we can't expect boys and girls to be old before their time.

Olivia. What generosity! But can you forget the many falsehoods, the dissimulation—

Croaker. You did indeed dissemble, you urchin, you; but where's the girl that won't dissemble for an husband! My wife and I had never been married, if we had not dissembled a little before hand!

Olivia. It shall be my future care never to put such generosity to a second trial. And as for the partner of my offence and folly, from his native honour, and the just sense he has of his duty, I can answer for him that—

Enter LEONTINE.

Leontine. Permit him thus to answer for himself. [*Kneeling.*] Thus, sir, let me speak my gratitude for this unmerited forgiveness. Yes, sir, this even exceeds all your former tenderness: I now can boast the most indulgent of fathers. The life he gave, compared to this, was but a trifling blessing!

Croaker. And, good sir, who sent for you, with that fine tragedy face and flourishing manner? I don't know what we have to do with your gratitude upon this occasion!

Leontine. How, sir! is it possible to be silent when so much oblig'd? Would you refuse me the pleasure of being grateful? Of adding my thanks to my Olivia's? Of sharing in the transports that you have thus occasion'd?

Croaker. Lord, sir, we can be happy enough, without your coming in to make up the party. I don't know what's the matter with the boy all this day; he has got into such a rhodomontade manner all the morning!

Leontine. But, Sir, I that have so large a part in the benefit, is it not my duty to shew my joy? Is the being admitted to your favour so slight an obligation? Is the happiness of marrying my Olivia so small a blessing?

Croaker. Marrying Olivia! marrying Olivia! marrying his own sister! Sure, the boy is out of his senses. His own sister!

Leontine. My sister!

Olivia [*Aside*]. Sister! How have I been mistaken!

Leontine [*Aside*]. Some curs'd mistake in all this I find.

Croaker. What does the booby mean, or has he any meaning? Eh, what do you mean, you blockhead, you?

Leontine. Mean, sir—why, sir—only when my sister is to be married, that I have the pleasure of marrying her, sir; that is, of giving her away, sir—I have made a point of it.

Croaker. O, is that all? "Give her away." You "have made a point of it." Then you had as good make a point of first giving away yourself, as I'm going to prepare the writings between you and Miss Richland this very minute. What a fuss is here about nothing! Why, what's the mat-

ter now? I thought I had made you, at least, as happy as
you could wish.

Olivia. O! yes, sir, very happy.

Croaker. Do you foresee any thing, child? You look
as if you did. I think if any thing was to be foreseen, I
have as sharp a look out as another: and yet I foresee
nothing.   [*Exit.*

LEONTINE, OLIVIA.

Olivia. What can it mean?

Leontine. He knows something, and yet for my life, I
can't tell what.

Olivia. It can't be the connexion between us, I'm pretty
certain.

Leontine. Whatever it be, my dearest, I'm resolv'd to
put it out of Fortune's power to repeat our mortification.
I'll haste, and prepare for our journey to Scotland this
very evening. My friend Honeywood has promis'd me his
advice and assistance. I'll go to him, and repose our distresses on his friendly bosom: and I know so much of his
honest heart, that if he can't relieve our uneasiness, he
will at least share them.   [*Exeunt.*

ACT THE THIRD

SCENE—*Young* HONEYWOOD'S *House*

BAILIFF, HONEYWOOD, FOLLOWER.

BAILIFF. Looky, sir, I have arrested as good men as you in
my time: no disparagement of you neither. Men that
would go forty guineas on a game of cribbage. I challenge
the town to shew a man in more genteeler practice than
myself!

Honeywood. Without all question, Mr.—I forget your
name, sir?

Bailiff. How can you forget what you never knew? he,
he, he!

Honeywood. May I beg leave to ask your name?

Bailiff. Yes, you may.

Honeywood. Then, pray, sir, what is your name, sir?

Bailiff. That I didn't promise to tell you. He, he, he! A

joke breaks no bones, as we say among us that practice
the law.

Honeywood. You may have reason for keeping it a
secret, perhaps?

Bailiff. The law does nothing without reason. I'm
asham'd to tell my name to no man, sir. If you can shew
cause, as why, upon a special capus, that I should prove
my name—But come, Timothy Twitch is my name. And,
now you know my name, what have you to say to that?

Honeywood. Nothing in the world, good Mr. Twitch,
but that I have a favour to ask, that's all.

Bailiff. Ay, favours are more easily asked than granted,
as we say among us that practice the law. I have taken an
oath against granting favours. Would you have me perjure
myself?

Honeywood. But my request will come recommended
in so strong a manner, as I believe you'll have no scruple
[*Pulling out his purse*]. The thing is only this: I believe I
shall be able to discharge this trifle in two or three days
at farthest; but as I would not have the affair known for
the world, I have thoughts of keeping you, and your good
friend here, about me, till the debt is discharged; for which
I shall be properly grateful.[42]

Bailiff. Oh! that's another maxum, and altogether within
my oath. For certain, if an honest man is to get any thing
by a thing, there's no reason why all things should not
be done in civility.

Honeywood. Doubtless, all trades must live, Mr. Twitch;
and your's is a necessary one.   [*Gives him money.*

Bailiff. Oh, your honour! I hope your honour takes
nothing amiss as I does, as I does nothing but my duty in
so doing. I'm sure no man can say I ever give a gentleman,
that was a gentleman, ill usage. If I saw that a gentleman
was a gentleman, I have taken money not to see him for
ten weeks together.

Honeywood. Tenderness is a virtue, Mr. Twitch.

Bailiff. Ay, sir, it's a perfect treasure. I love to see a
gentleman with a tender heart. I don't know, but I think
I have a tender heart myself. If all that I have lost by my
heart was put together, it would make a—but no matter
for that.

[42] There is an anecdote of Steele which may have suggested
this expedient of putting the bailiffs into livery. See *Richard
Steele, English Worthies*, 1886, p. 222.

Honeywood. Don't account it lost, Mr. Twitch. The ingratitude of the world can never deprive us of the conscious happiness of having acted with humanity ourselves.

Bailiff. Humanity, sir, is a jewel. Its better than gold. I love humanity. People may say that we, in our way, have no humanity; but I'll shew you my humanity this moment. There's my follower here, little Flanigan, with a wife and four children; a guinea or two would be more to him than twice as much to another. Now, as I can't shew him any humanity myself, I must beg leave you'll do it for me.

Honeywood. I assure you, Mr. Twitch, your's is a most powerful recommendation.

[*Giving money to the* FOLLOWER.

Bailiff. Sir, you're a gentleman. I see you know what to do with your money. But, to business: we are to be with you here as your friends, I suppose. But set in case company comes—Little Flanigan here, to be sure, has a good face; a very good face: but then, he is a little seedy, as we say among us that practice the law. Not well in cloaths. Smoke the pocket holes.

Honeywood. Well, that shall be remedied without delay.

Enter Servant.

Servant. Sir, Miss Richland is below.

Honeywood. How unlucky! Detain her a moment. We must improve, my good friend, little Mr. Flanigan's appearance first. Here, let Mr. Flanigan have a suit of my cloaths—quick—the brown and silver—Do you hear?

Servant. That your honour gave away to the begging gentleman that makes verses, because it was as good as new.

Honeywood. The white and gold, then.

Servant. That, your honour, I made bold to sell, because it was good for nothing.

Honeywood. Well, the first that comes to hand, then. The blue and gold. I believe Mr. Flanigan will look best in blue.   [*Exit* FLANIGAN.

Bailiff. Rabbit me, but little Flanigan will look well in any thing. Ah, if your honour knew that bit of flesh as well as I do, you'd be perfectly in love with him. There's not a prettyer scout in the four counties after a shycock than he. Scents like a hound; sticks like a weazle. He was master of the ceremonies to the black queen of Moroco[43] when I took him to follow me. [*Re-enter* FLANIGAN.] Heh, ecod, I think he looks so well that I don't care if I have a suit from the same place for myself.

Honeywood. Well, well, I hear the lady coming! Dear Mr. Twitch, I beg you'll give your friend directions not to speak. As for yourself, I know you will say nothing without being directed.

Bailiff. Never you fear me, I'll shew the lady that I have something to say for myself as well as another. One man has one way of talking, and another man has another, that's all the difference between them.

Enter MISS RICHLAND *and her* MAID.

Miss Richland. You'll be surprised, sir, with this visit. But you know I'm yet to thank you for chusing my little library.

Honeywood. Thanks, madam, are unnecessary, as it was I that was obliged by your commands. Chairs here. Two of my very good friends, Mr. Twitch and Mr. Flanigan. Pray, gentlemen, sit without ceremony.

Miss Richland [*Aside*]. Who can these odd-looking men be? I fear it is as I was informed. It must be so.

Bailiff [*After a pause*]. Pretty weather, very pretty weather for the time of the year, madam.

Follower. Very good circuit weather in the country.

Honeywood. You officers are generally favourites among the ladies. My friends, madam, have been upon very disagreeable duty, I assure you. The fair should, in some measure, recompence the toils of the brave.

Miss Richland. Our officers do indeed deserve every favour. The gentlemen are in the marine service, I presume, sir?

Honeywood. Why, madam, they do—occasionally serve in the Fleet, madam! A dangerous service!

Miss Richland. I'm told so. And I own, it has often surprised me, that, while we have had so many instances of bravery there, we have had so few of wit at home to praise it.

[43] This probably means that Mr. Flanigan, like the author's strolling player, had been employed in connection with a puppet-show. "The court of the Black king of Morocco" at Sudrick Fair is referred to in *Essays*, 1766, p. 236.

Honeywood. I grant, madam, that our poets have not written as our soldiers[44] have fought; but they have done all they could, and Hawke or Amherst[45] could do no more.

Miss Richland. I'm quite displeased when I see a fine subject spoiled by a dull writer.

Honeywood. We should not be so severe against dull writers, madam. It is ten to one, but the dullest writer exceeds the most rigid French critic who presumes to despise him.

Follower. Damn the French, the parle vous, and all that belongs to them!

Miss Richland. Sir!

Honeywood. Ha, ha, ha, honest Mr. Flanigan! A true English officer, madam; he's not contented with beating the French, but he will scold them too.

Miss Richland. Yet, Mr. Honeywood, this does not convince me but that severity in criticism is necessary. It was our first adopting the severity of French taste that has brought them in turn to taste us.

Bailiff. Taste us! By the Lord, madam, they devour us! Give Monseers but a taste, and I'll be damn'd but they come in for a bellyful!

Miss Richland. Very extraordinary, this.

Follower. But very true. What makes the bread rising: the parle vous that devour us. What makes the mutton fivepence a pound: the parle vous that eat it up. What makes the beer three pence halfpenny a pot—

Honeywood. Ah, the vulgar rogues, all will be out! Right, gentlemen, very right, upon my word, and quite to the purpose. They draw a parallel, madam, between the mental taste and that of our senses. We are injur'd as much by French severity in the one as by French rapacity in the other. That's their meaning.

Miss Richland. Tho' I don't see the force of the parallel, yet I'll own that we should sometimes pardon books, as we do our friends, that have now and then agreeable absurdities to recommend them.

Bailiff. That's all my eye! The King only can pardon, as the law says: for set in case—

[44] This is the reading of the octavos; but some later editions read, "sailors."

[45] Admiral Hawke, 1705-81, defeated the French in Quiberon Bay, 1759; General Amherst, 1717-97, captured Louisburg, Ticonderoga, etc.

Honeywood. I'm quite of your opinion, sir! I see the whole drift of your argument. Yes, certainly our presuming to pardon any work is arrogating a power that belongs to another. If all have power to condemn, what writer can be free?

Bailiff. By his habus corpus. His habus corpus can set him free at any time. For set in case—

Honeywood. I'm obliged to you, sir, for the hint. If, madam, as my friend observes, our laws are so careful of a gentleman's person, sure we ought to be equally careful of his dearer part, his fame.

Follower. Ay, but if so be a man's nabb'd, you know—

Honeywood. Mr. Flanigan, if you spoke[46] for ever, you could not improve the last observation. For my own part, I think it conclusive.

Bailiff. As for the matter of that, mayhap—

Honeywood. Nay, sir, give me leave in this instance to be positive. For where is the necessity of censuring works without genius, which must shortly sink of themselves: what is it but aiming our unnecessary blow against a victim already under the hands of justice?

Bailiff. Justice! O, by the elevens, if you talk about justice, I think I am at home there; for, in a course of law—

Honeywood. My dear Mr. Twitch, I discern what you'd be at perfectly, and I believe the lady must be sensible of the art with which it is introduced. I suppose you perceive the meaning, madam, of his "course of law?"

Miss Richland. I protest, sir, I do not. I perceive only that you answer one gentleman before he has finished, and the other before he has well begun!

Bailiff. Madam, you are a gentlewoman, and I will make the matter out. This here question is about severity and justice, and pardon, and the like of they. Now, to explain the thing—

Honeywood [*Aside*]. O! curse your explanations.

Enter Servant.

Servant. Mr. Leontine, sir, below, desires to speak with you upon earnest business.

Honeywood [*Aside*]. That's lucky.—Dear madam, you'll excuse me, and my good friends here, for a few

[46] *Spoke.* O1, spake; Brit. Mu. O1 speak (Dobson); O2, spoke.

minutes. There are books, madam, to amuse you. Come, gentlemen, you know I make no ceremony with such friends. After you, sir. Excuse me. Well, if I must. But I know your natural politeness!

Bailiff. Before and behind, you know.

Follower. Ay, ay, before and behind, before and behind!

[*Exeunt* HONEYWOOD, BAILIFF, *and* FOLLOWER.

Miss Richland. What can all this mean, Garnet?

Garnet. Mean, madam? why, what should it mean but what Mr. Lofty sent you here to see? These people he calls officers are officers sure enough: sheriff's officers; bailiffs, madam!

Miss Richland. Ay, it is certainly so. Well, tho' his perplexities are far from giving me pleasure, yet, I own, there's something very ridiculous in them, and a just punishment for his dissimulation.

Garnet. And so they are. But I wonder, madam, that the lawyer you just employed to pay his debts, and set him free, has not done it by this time. He ought at least to have been here before now. But lawyers are always more ready to get a man into troubles than out of them!

Enter SIR WILLIAM.

Sir William. For Miss Richland to undertake setting him free, I own, was quite unexpected. It has totally unhinged my schemes to reclaim him. Yet, it gives me pleasure to find that, among a number of worthless friendships, he has made one acquisition of real value; for there must be some softer passion on her side that prompts this generosity. Ha! here before me: I'll endeavor to sound her affections. Madam, as I am the person that have had some demands upon the gentleman of this house, I hope you'll excuse me, if, before I enlarge him, I wanted to see yourself.

Miss Richland. The precaution was very unnecessary, sir! I suppose your wants were only such as my agent had power to satisfy.

Sir William. Partly, madam. But I was also willing you should be fully apprized of the character of the gentleman you intended to serve.

Miss Richland. It must come, sir, with a very ill grace from you. To censure it, after what you have done, would look like malice; and to speak favourably of a character you have oppressed would be impeaching your own. And, sure, his tenderness, his humanity, his universal friendship may atone for many faults!

Sir William. That friendship, madam, which is exerted in too wide a sphere becomes totally useless. Our bounty, like a drop of water, disappears when diffused too widely. They who pretend most to this universal benevolence are either deceivers or dupes. Men who desire to cover their private ill-nature by a pretended regard for all; or men who, reasoning themselves into false feelings, are more earnest in pursuit of splendid than of useful virtues.

Miss Richland. I am surprised, sir, to hear one who has probably been a gainer by the folly of others so severe in his censure of it.

Sir William. Whatever I may have gained by folly, madam, you see I am willing to prevent your losing by it.

Miss Richland. Your cares for me, sir, are unnecessary. I always suspect those services which are denied where they are wanted, and offered, perhaps, in hopes of a refusal. No, sir, my directions have been given, and I insist upon their being complied with.

Sir William. Thou amiable woman! I can no longer contain the expressions of my gratitude, my pleasure. You see before you one who has been equally careful of his interest: one who has for some time been a concealed spectator of his follies, and only punished in hopes to reclaim them—His uncle!

Miss Richland. Sir William Honeywood! You amaze me. How shall I conceal my confusion? I fear, sir, you'll think I have been too forward in my services. I confess I—

Sir William. Don't make any apologies, madam. I only find myself unable to repay the obligation. And yet, I have been trying my interest of late to serve you. Having learnt, madam, that you had some demands upon Government, I have, tho' unasked, been your solicitor there.

Miss Richland. Sir, I'm infinitely obliged to your intentions. But my guardian has employed another gentleman who assures him of success.

Sir William. Who, the important little man that visits here! Trust me, madam, he's quite contemptible among men in power, and utterly unable to serve you. Mr. Lofty's promises are much better known to people of fashion than his person, I assure you.

Miss Richland. How have we been deceived! As sure as can be, here he comes.

Sir William. Does he? Remember, I'm to continue unknown. My return to England has not as yet been made public. With what impudence he enters!

Enter LOFTY.

Lofty. Let the chariot—let my chariot drive off, I'll visit to his Grace's in a chair. Miss Richland here before me! Punctual, as usual, to the calls of humanity. I'm very sorry, madam, things of this kind should happen, especially to a man I have shewn every where, and carried amongst us as a particular acquaintance.

Miss Richland. I find, sir, you have the art of making the misfortunes of others your own.

Lofty. My dear madam, what can a private man like me do? One man can't do every thing; and then, I do so much in this way every day: let me see, something considerable might be done for him by subscription; it could not fail if I carried the list. I'll undertake to set down a brace of dukes, two dozen lords, and half the lower House, at my own peril!

Sir William. And after all, its more than probable, sir, he might reject the offer of such powerful patronage.

Lofty. Then, madam, what can we do? You know I never make promises. In truth, I once or twice tried to do something with him in the way of business; but, as I often told his uncle, Sir William Honeywood, the man was utterly impracticable.

Sir William. His uncle! Then that gentleman, I suppose, is a particular friend of yours.

Lofty. Meaning me, sir?—Yes, madam, as I often said, "My dear Sir William, you are sensible I would do any thing as far as my poor interest goes to serve your family; but what can be done? there's no procuring first rate places for ninth rate abilities?"

Miss Richland. I have heard of Sir William Honeywood; he's abroad in employment; he confided in your judgment, I suppose.

Lofty. Why, yes, madam; I believe Sir William had some reason to confide in my judgment; one little reason, perhaps.

Miss Richland. Pray, sir, what was it?

Lofty. Why, madam,—but let it go no further,—it was I procured him his place.

Sir William. Did you, sir?

Lofty. Either you or I, sir.

Miss Richland. This, Mr. Lofty, was very kind, indeed.

Lofty. I did love him, to be sure; he had some amusing qualities; no man was fitter to be toast-master to a club, or had a better head.

Miss Richland. A better head?

Lofty. Ay, at a bottle. To be sure, he was as dull as a choice spirit;[47] but hang it, he was grateful, very grateful; and gratitude hides a multitude of faults!

Sir William. He might have reason, perhaps. His place is pretty considerable, I'm told.

Lofty. A trifle, a mere trifle, among us men of business. The truth is, he wanted dignity to fill up a greater.

Sir William. Dignity of person, do you mean, sir? I'm told he's much about my size and figure, sir.

Lofty. Ay, tall enough for a marching regiment; but then he wanted a something—a consequence of form—a kind of a—I believe the lady perceives my meaning.

Miss Richland. O perfectly; you courtiers can do any thing, I see!

Lofty. My dear madam, all this is but a mere exchange; we do greater things for one another every day. Why, as thus, now: let me suppose you the first lord of the Treasury; you have an employment in you that I want; I have a place in me that you want; do me here, do you there: interest of both sides, few words, flat, done and done, and its over.

Sir William [*Aside*]. A thought strikes me.—Now you mention Sir William Honeywood, madam,—and as he seems, sir, an acquaintance of yours,—you'll be glad to hear he's arrived from Italy; I had it from a friend who knows him as well as he does me, and you may depend on my information.

Lofty [*Aside*]. The devil he is! If I had known that, we should not have been quite so well acquainted.

Sir William. He is certainly return'd; and as this gentleman is a friend of yours, he can be of signal service to

47 Cf. The dull Club of Choice Spirits in *Essays*, 1765, No. IV. Dickens, in the *Old Curiosity Shop*, makes Mr. Swiveller tell Quilp the dwarf that he is not a "choice spirit" (ch. xxiii).

us by introducing me to him; there are some papers rela-
tive to your affairs that require dispatch and his inspection.

Miss Richland. This gentleman, Mr. Lofty, is a person
employed in my affairs: I know you'll serve us.

Lofty. My dear madam, I live but to serve you. Sir
William shall even wait upon him, if you think proper to
command it.

Sir William. That would be quite unnecessary.

Lofty. Well, we must introduce you, then. Call upon
me—let me see—ay, in two days.

Sir William. Now, or the opportunity will be lost for
ever.

Lofty. Well, if it must be now, now let it be.[48] But,
damn it, that's unfortunate; my Lord Grig's curs'd Pen-
sacola business comes on this very hour, and I'm engaged
to attend—another time—

Sir William. A short letter to Sir William will do.

Lofty. You shall have it; yet, in my opinion, a letter
is a very bad way of going to work; face to face, that's
my way.

Sir William. The letter, sir, will do quite as well.

Lofty. Zounds, sir, do you pretend to direct me; direct
me in the business of office? Do you know me, sir? who
am I?

Miss Richland. Dear Mr. Lofty, this request is not so
much his as mine; if my commands—but you despise my
power.

Lofty. Delicate creature! your commands could even
controul a debate at midnight; to a power so constitutional,
I am all obedience and tranquility. He shall have a letter;
where is my secretary? Dubardieu! And yet, I protest
I don't like this way of doing business. I think if I spoke
first to Sir William—But you will have it so.

[*Exit with* Miss Richland.

Sir William *alone.*

Sir William. Ha, ha, ha! This, too, is one of my nephew's
hopeful associates. O vanity, thou constant deceiver, how
do all thy efforts to exalt serve but to sink us. Thy false
colourings, like those employed to heighten beauty, only
seem to mend that bloom which they contribute to de-
stroy. I'm not displeased at this interview; exposing this

---

[48] *Now let it be.* In O1 *let* is missing.

fellow's impudence to the contempt it deserves may be of use to my design; at least, if he can reflect, it will be of use to himself.

Enter JARVIS.

Sir William. How now, Jarvis, where's your master, my nephew?

Jarvis. At his wits end, I believe; he's scarce gotten out of one scrape, but he's running his head into another.

Sir William. How so?

Jarvis. The house has but just been cleared of the bailiffs, and now he's again engaging tooth and nail in assisting old Croaker's son to patch up a clandestine match with the young lady that passes in the house for his sister!

Sir William. Ever busy to serve others.

Jarvis. Ay, anybody but himself. The young couple, it seems, are just setting out for Scotland, and he supplies them with money for the journey.

Sir William. Money! How is he able to supply others, who has scarce any for himself?

Jarvis. Why, there it is; he has no money, that's true; but then, as he never said no to any request in his life, he has given them a bill drawn by a friend of his upon a merchant in the city, which I am to get chang'd; for you must know that I am to go with them to Scotland myself.

Sir William. How!

Jarvis. It seems the young gentleman is obliged to take a different road from his mistress, as he is to call upon an uncle of his that lives out of the way, in order to prepare a place for their reception, when they return; so they have borrowed me from my master, as the properest person to attend the young lady down.

Sir William. To the land of matrimony! A pleasant journey, Jarvis.

Jarvis. Ay, but I'm only to have all the fatigues on't.

Sir William. Well, it may be shorter and less fatiguing than you imagine. I know but too much of the young lady's family and connexions, whom I have seen abroad. I have also discover'd that Miss Richland is not indifferent to my thoughtless nephew; and will endeavour, tho' I fear in vain, to establish that connexion. But, come, the letter I wait for must be almost finish'd; I'll let you further into my intentions in the next room. [*Exeunt.*

ACT THE FOURTH

scene—Croaker's *House*

Lofty.

LOFTY. Well, sure the devil's in me of late, for running my head into such defiles as nothing but a genius like my own could draw me from. I was formerly contented to husband out my places and pensions with some degree of frugality; but, curse it, of late I have given away the whole Court Register in less time than they could print the title page; yet, hang it, why scruple a lie or two to come at a fine girl when I every day tell a thousand for nothing. Ha! Honeywood here before me. Could Miss Richland have set him at liberty?

Enter HONEYWOOD.

Mr. Honeywood, I'm glad to see you abroad again. I find my concurrence was not necessary in your unfortunate affairs. I had put things in a train to do your business; but it is not for me to say what I intended doing.

Honeywood. It was unfortunate, indeed, sir. But what adds to my uneasiness is, that while you seem to be acquainted with my misfortune, I, myself, continue still a stranger to my benefactor.

Lofty. How! not know the friend that served you?

Honeywood. Can't guess at the person.

Lofty. Enquire.

Honeywood. I have, but all I can learn is, that he chuses to remain concealed, and that all enquiry must be fruitless.

Lofty. Must be fruitless?

Honeywood. Absolutely fruitless.

Lofty. Sure of that?

Honeywood. Very sure.

Lofty. Then I'll be damn'd if you shall ever know it from me.

Honeywood. How, sir!

Lofty. I suppose, now, Mr. Honeywood, you think my rent-roll very considerable, and that I have vast sums of money to throw away; I know you do. The world, to be sure, says such things of me.

Honeywood. The world, by what I learn, is no stranger to your generosity. But where does this tend?

Lofty. To nothing; nothing in the world. The town, to be sure, when it makes such a thing as me the subject of conversation has asserted that I never yet patronized a man of merit.

Honeywood. I have heard instances to the contrary, even from yourself.

Lofty. Yes, Honeywood, and there are instances to the contrary that you shall never hear from myself.

Honeywood. Ha, dear sir, permit me to ask you but one question.

Lofty. Sir, ask me no questions: I say, sir, ask me no questions; I'll be damn'd if I answer them!

Honeywood. I will ask no further. My friend, my benefactor, it is, it must be here, that I am indebted for freedom, for honour. Yes, thou worthiest of men, from the beginning I suspected it, but was afraid to return thanks; which, if undeserved, might seem reproaches.

Lofty. I protest I don't understand all this, Mr. Honeywood! You treat me very cavalierly. I do assure you, sir. —Blood, sir, can't a man be permitted to enjoy the luxury of his own feelings without all this parade?

Honeywood. Nay, do not attempt to conceal an action that adds to your honour. Your looks, your air, your manner, all confess it.

Lofty. Confess it, sir! Torture itself, sir, shall never bring me to confess it. Mr. Honeywood, I have admitted you upon terms of friendship. Don't let us fall out; make me happy, and let this be buried in oblivion. You know I hate ostentation; you know I do. Come, come, Honeywood, you know I always lov'd to be a friend, and not a patron. I beg this may make no kind of distance between us. Come, come, you and I must be more familiar —Indeed we must.

Honeywood. Heavens! Can I ever repay such friendship! Is there any way! Thou best of men, can I ever return the obligation?

Lofty. A bagatelle, a mere bagatelle. But I see your heart is labouring to be grateful. You shall be grateful. It would be cruel to disappoint you.

Honeywood. How! Teach me the manner. Is there any way?

Lofty. From this moment you're mine. Yes, my friend, you shall know it—I'm in love!

Honeywood. And can I assist you?

Lofty. Nobody so well.

Honeywood. In what manner? I'm all impatience.

Lofty. You shall make love for me.

Honeywood. And to whom shall I speak in your favour?

Lofty. To a lady with whom you have great interest, I assure you. Miss Richland.

Honeywood. Miss Richland!

Lofty. Yes, Miss Richland. She has struck the blow up to the hilt in my bosom, by Jupiter!

Honeywood. Heavens! was ever any thing more unfortunate! It is too much to be endur'd.

Lofty. Unfortunate, indeed! And yet I can endure it, till you have opened the affair to her for me. Between ourselves, I think she likes me. I'm not apt to boast, but I think she does.

Honeywood. Indeed! But do you know the person you apply to?

Lofty. Yes, I know you are her friend and mine: that's enough. To you, therefore, I commit the success of my passion. I'll say no more, let friendship do the rest. I have only to add, that if at any time my little interest can be of service,—but, hang it, I'll make no promises,—you know my interest is your's at any time. No apologies, my friend, I'll not be answered, it shall be so.   [*Exit.*

Honeywood. Open, generous, unsuspecting man! He little thinks that I love her too; and with such an ardent passion!—But then it was ever but a vain and hopeless one;[49] my torment, my persecution! What shall I do! Love, friendship, a hopeless passion, a deserving friend! Love, that has been my tormentor; a friend, that has, perhaps, distress'd himself to serve me. It shall be so. Yes, I will discard the fondling hope from my bosom, and exert all my influence in his favour. And yet to see her in the possession of another!—Insupportable. But then to betray a generous, trusting friend!—Worse, worse. Yes, I'm resolv'd. Let me but be the instrument of their happiness, and then quit a country where I must for ever despair of finding my own.   [*Exit.*

[49] *Hopeless one . . . Love, friendship.* O1 reads, *Hopeless one. My torment, my persecution, what shall I do!*

Enter OLIVIA *and* GARNET, *who carries a milliner's box.*

Olivia. Dear me, I wish this journey were over. No news of Jarvis yet? I believe the old peevish creature delays purely to vex me.

Garnet. Why, to be sure, madam, I did hear him say a little snubbing before marriage would teach you to bear it the better afterwards.

Olivia. To be gone a full hour, tho' he had only to get a bill changed in the city! How provoking!

Garnet. I'll lay my life, Mr. Leontine, that had twice as much to do, is setting off by this time from his inn; and here you are left behind.

Olivia. Well, let us be prepar'd for his coming, however. Are you sure you have omitted nothing, Garnet?

Garnet. Not a stick, madam—all's here. Yet I wish you could take the white and silver to be married in. It's the worst luck in the world in anything but white. I knew one Bett Stubbs, of our town, that was married in red; and, as sure as eggs is eggs, the bridegroom and she had a miff before morning.

Olivia. No matter. I'm all impatience till we are out of the house.

Garnet. Bless me, madam, I had almost forgot the wedding-ring!—The sweet little thing—I don't think it would go on my little finger. And what if I put in a gentleman's night-cap, in case of necessity, madam? But here's Jarvis.

Enter JARVIS.

Olivia. O, Jarvis, are you come at last? We have been ready this half hour. Now let's be going. Let us fly.

Jarvis. Aye, to Jericho! for we shall have no going to Scotland this bout, I fancy.

Olivia. How! What's the matter?

Jarvis. Money, money, is the matter, madam. We have got no money. What the plague do you send me of your fool's errand for? My master's bill upon the city is not worth a rush. Here it is; Mrs. Garnet may pin up her hair with it.

Olivia. Undone! How could Honeywood serve us so! What shall we do? Can't we go without it?

Jarvis. Go to Scotland without money! [50] To Scotland

[50] This is probably a cheap jibe at the impossibility of doing anything in North Britain without paying for it.

without money! Lord how some people understand ge-
ography! We might as well set sail for Patagonia upon a
cork jacket.

Olivia. Such a disappointment! What a base, insincere
man was your master, to serve us in this manner. Is this
his good nature?

Jarvis. Nay, don't talk ill of my master, madam. I won't
bear to hear any body talk ill of him but myself.

Garnet. Bless us! now I think on't, madam, you need
not be under any uneasiness: I saw Mr. Leontine receive
forty guineas from his father just before he set out, and
he can't yet have left the inn. A short letter will reach
him there.

Olivia. Well remember'd, Garnet; I'll write immediately.
How's this! Bless me, my hand trembles so I can't write
a word. Do you write, Garnet; and, upon second thought,
it will be better from you.

Garnet. Truly, madam, I write and indite but poorly.
I never was kute at my larning. But I'll do what I can
to please you. Let me see. All out of my own head,
I suppose?

Olivia. Whatever you please.

Garnet [*Writing*]. "Muster Croaker"—Twenty guineas,
madam?

Olivia. Ay, twenty will do.

Garnet. "At the bar of the Talbot till call'd for. Expedition—will be blown up—All of a flame—Quick, dispatch—Cupid, the little God of Love"—I conclude it,
madam, with Cupid; I love to see a love letter end like
poetry.[51]

Olivia. Well, well, what you please, any thing. But how
shall we send it? I can trust none of the servants of this
family.

Garnet. Odso, madam, Mr. Honeywood's butler is in
the next room; he's a dear, sweet man; he'll do any thing
for me.

Jarvis. He! the dog, he'll certainly commit some blunder.
He's drunk and sober ten times a day!

Olivia. No matter. Fly, Garnet; any body we can trust
will do. [*Exit* GARNET.] Well, Jarvis, now we can have
nothing more to interrupt us. You may take up the things

---

[51] *I love . . . end like poetry.* From chapter xxxiii. of the
Pickwick Papers, this would also seem to have been the view
of Mr. Samuel Weller.

and carry them on to the inn. Have you no hands, Jarvis?

Jarvis. Soft and fair, young lady. You that are going to be married think things can never be done too fast: but we that are old, and know what we are about, must elope methodically, madam.

Olivia. Well, sure, if my indiscretions were to be done over again—

Jarvis. My life for it you would do them ten times over.

Olivia. What will you talk so? If you knew how un-happy they make me—

Jarvis. Very unhappy, no doubt: I was once just as unhappy when I was going to be married myself. I'll tell you a story about that—

Olivia. A story! when I'm all impatience to be away! Was there ever such a dilatory creature!—

Jarvis. Well, madam, if we must march, why we will march; that's all. Tho', odds bobs, we have still forgot one thing we should never travel without—a case of good razors, and a box of shaving-powder. But no matter, I believe we shall be pretty well shaved by the way. [*Going.*

Enter GARNET.

Garnet. Undone, undone, madam! Ah, Mr. Jarvis, you said right enough. As sure as death, Mr. Honeywood's rogue of a drunken butler drop'd the letter before he went ten yards from the door. There's old Croaker has just pick'd it up, and is this moment reading it to himself in the hall!

Olivia. Unfortunate! We shall be discover'd!

Garnet. No, madam; don't be uneasy, he can make neither head nor tail of it. To be sure he looks as if he was broke loose from Bedlam about it, but he can't find what it means for all that. O Lud, he is coming this way all in the horrors!

Olivia. Then let us leave the house this instant, for fear he should ask farther questions. In the mean time, Garnet, do you write and send off just such another.
[*Exeunt.*

Enter CROAKER.

Croaker. Death and destruction! Are all the horrors of air, fire and water to be levelled only at me! Am I only to be singled out for gunpowder-plots, combustibles, and conflagration! Here it is—an incendiary letter drop'd at

my door. *To Muster Croaker, these, with speed.* Ay, ay,
plain enough the direction: all in the genuine incendiary
spelling, and as cramp as the devil. *With speed.* O, confound your speed. But let me read it once more. [*Reads.*]
*Mustar Croakar as sone as yoew see this leve twenty
gunnes at the bar of the Talboot tell caled for or yowe
and yower experetion will be al blown up!* Ah, but too
plain! Blood and gunpowder in every line of it. Blown
up! murderous dog! All blown up! Heavens! what have
I and my poor family done, to be all blown up? [*Reads.*]
Our pockets are low, and money we must have. Ay, there's
the reason; they'll blow us up, because they have got low
pockets. [*Reads.*] *It is but a short time you have to consider; for if this takes wind, the house will quickly be all
of a flame.* Inhuman monsters! blow us up, and then burn
us. The earthquake at Lisbon was but a bonfire to it!
[*Reads.*] *Make quick despatch, and so no more at present.
But may Cupid, the little God of Love, go with you
wherever you go.* The little God of Love! Cupid, the
little God of Love go with me! Go you to the devil, you
and your little Cupid together; I'm so frightened, I scarce
know whether I sit, stand, or go. Perhaps this moment
I'm treading on lighted matches, blazing brimstone and
barrels of gunpowder. They are preparing to blow me
up into the clouds. Murder! We shall be all burnt in our
beds; we shall be all burnt in our beds.[52]

Enter MISS RICHLAND.

Miss Richland. Lord, sir, what's the matter?

Croaker. Murder's the matter. We shall be all blown
up in our beds before morning!

Miss Richland. I hope not, sir.

Croaker. What signifies what you hope, madam, when
I have a certificate of it here in my hand? Will nothing
alarm my family? Sleeping and eating, sleeping and eating
is the only work from morning till night in my house.
My insensible crew could sleep, tho' rock'd by an earthquake; and fry beef steaks at a volcano!

Miss Richland. But, sir, you have alarmed them so often
already, we have nothing but earthquakes, famines,
plagues, and mad dogs from year's end to year's end. You
remember, sir, it is not above a month ago, you assur'd

us of a conspiracy among the bakers, to poison us in our bread; and so kept the whole family a week upon potatoes.

Croaker. And potatoes were too good for them. But why do I stand talking here with a girl when I should be facing the enemy without? Here, John, Nicodemus, search the house. Look into the cellars, to see if there be any combustibles below; and above, in the apartments, that no matches be thrown in at the windows. Let all the fires be put out, and let the engine be drawn out in the yard, to play upon the house in case of necessity.   [*Exit.*

Miss Richland *alone.*

Miss Richland. What can he mean by all this? Yet, why should I enquire, when he alarms us in this manner almost every day? But Honeywood has desired an interview with me in private. What can he mean; or, rather, what means this palpitation at his approach? It is the first time he ever shewed any thing in his conduct that seem'd particular. Sure he cannot mean to—but he's here.

Enter HONEYWOOD.

Honeywood. I presum'd to solicit this interview, madam, before I left town, to be permitted—

Miss Richland. Indeed! Leaving town, sir?—

Honeywood. Yes, madam; perhaps the kingdom. I have presumed, I say, to desire the favour of this interview—in order to disclose something which our long friendship prompts. And yet my fears—

Miss Richland [*Aside*]. His fears! What are his fears to mine!—We have indeed been long acquainted, sir; very long. If I remember, our first meeting was at the French Ambassador's.—Do you recollect how you were pleas'd to rally me upon my complexion there?

Honeywood. Perfectly, madam; I presum'd to reprove you for painting: but your warmer blushes soon convinc'd the company that the colouring was all from nature.

Miss Richland. And yet you only meant it, in your good natur'd way, to make me pay a compliment to myself. In the same manner you danc'd that night with the most awkward woman in company, because you saw nobody else would take her out.

Honeywood. Yes; and was rewarded the next night by

dancing with the finest woman in company, whom every body wish'd to take out.

Miss Richland. Well, sir, if you thought so then, I fear your judgment has since corrected the errors of a first impression. We generally shew to most advantage at first. Our sex are like poor tradesmen, that put all their best goods to be seen at the windows.

Honeywood. The first impression, madam, did indeed deceive me. I expected to find a woman with all the faults of conscious, flattered beauty. I expected to find her vain and insolent. But every day has since taught me that it is possible to possess sense without pride, and beauty without affection.

Miss Richland. This, sir, is a style very unusual with Mr. Honeywood; and I should be glad to know why he thus attempts to increase that vanity which his own lessons have[53] taught me to despise.

Honeywood. I ask pardon, madam. Yet, from our long friendship, I presumed I might have some right to offer, without offence, what you may refuse without offending.

Miss Richland. Sir! I beg you'd reflect; tho', I fear, I shall scarce have any power to refuse a request of yours; yet, you may precipitate: consider, sir.

Honeywood. I own my rashness; but, as I plead the cause of friendship, of one who loves—Don't be alarmed, madam—who loves you with the most ardent passion; whose whole happiness is placed in you—

Miss Richland. I fear, sir, I shall never find whom you mean by this description of him.

Honeywood. Ah, madam, it but too plainly points him out; tho' he should be too humble himself to urge his pretensions, or you too modest to understand them.

Miss Richland. Well; it would be affectation any longer to pretend ignorance; and, I will own, sir, I have long been prejudiced in his favour. It was but natural to wish to make his heart mine, as he seem'd himself ignorant of its value.

Honeywood [*Aside*]. I see she always lov'd him!—I find, madam, you're already sensible of his worth, his passion. How happy is my friend, to be the favourite of one with such sense to distinguish merit, and such beauty to reward it!

Miss Richland. Your friend, sir! What friend?

[53] O1-O3, hath.

Honeywood. My best friend—my friend Mr. Lofty, madam.

Miss Richland. He, sir!

Honeywood. Yes, he, madam! He is, indeed, what your warmest wishes might have form'd him. And to his other qualities, he adds that of the most passionate regard for you.

Miss Richland. Amazement!—No more of this, I beg you, sir.

Honeywood. I see your confusion, madam, and know how to interpret it. And since I so plainly read the language of your heart, shall I make my friend happy by communicating your sentiments?

Miss Richland. By no means.

Honeywood. Excuse me, I must; I know you desire it.

Miss Richland. Mr. Honeywood, let me tell you, that you wrong my sentiments and yourself. When I first applied to your friendship, I expected advice and assistance; but now, sir, I see that it is vain to expect happiness from him who has been so bad an œconomist of his own; and that I must disclaim his friendship who ceases to be a friend to himself.   [*Exit.*

Honeywood. How is this! She has confessed she lov'd him, and yet she seemed to part in displeasure. Can I have done any thing to reproach myself with? No; I believe not; yet, after all, these things should not be done by a third person; I should have spared her confusion. My friendship carried me a little too far.

Enter CROAKER, *with the letter in his hand, and*
MRS. CROAKER.

Mrs. Croaker. Ha, ha, ha! And so, my dear, it's your supreme wish that I should be quite wretched on this occasion? Ha, ha!

Croaker [*Mimicking*]. Ha, ha, ha! and so, my dear, it's your supreme pleasure to give me no better consolation?

Mrs. Croaker. Positively, my dear, what is this incendiary stuff and trumpery to me? Our house may travel thro' the air like the house of Loretto[54] for ought I care, if I'm to be miserable in it.

[54] The *Santa* or *Santissima Casa* (a house alleged to have been occupied by the Virgin Mary at Nazareth) is said to have made other miraculous aerial excursions before it settled finally in 1291 at Loretto in Italy (Province of Ancona).

Croaker. Would to Heaven it were converted into an house of correction for your benefit. Have we not every thing to alarm us? Perhaps, this very moment the tragedy is beginning?

Mrs. Croaker. Then let us reserve our distress till the rising of the curtain, or give them the money they want, and have done with them.

Croaker. Give them my money!—And pray, what right have they to my money?

Mrs. Croaker. And pray, what right then have you to my good humour?

Croaker. And so your good humour advises me to part with my money? Why, then, to tell your good humour a piece of my mind, I'd sooner part with my wife! Here's Mr. Honeywood; see what he'll say to it. My dear Honeywood, look at this incendiary letter dropped at my door. It will freeze you with terror; and yet lovey here can read it—can read it, and laugh!

Mrs. Croaker. Yes, and so will Mr. Honeywood.

Croaker. If he does, I'll suffer to be hanged the next minute in the rogue's place, that's all!

Mrs. Croaker. Speak, Mr. Honeywood; is there any thing more foolish than my husband's fright upon this occasion?

Honeywood. It would not become me to decide, madam; but doubtless, the greatness of his terrors now will but invite them to renew their villainy another time.

Mrs. Croaker. I told you, he'd be of my opinion.

Croaker. How, sir! do you maintain that I should lie down under such an injury, and shew, neither by my tears, or complaints,[55] that I have something of the spirit of a man in me?

Honeywood. Pardon me, sir. You ought to make the loudest complaints, if you desire redress. The surest way to have redress is to be earnest in the pursuit of it.

Croaker. Ay, whose opinion is he of now?

Mrs. Croaker. But don't you think that laughing off our fears is the best way?

Honeywood. What is the best, madam, few can say; but I'll maintain it to be a very wise way.

Croaker. But we're talking of the best. Surely the best

[55] *Tears, or complaints* in octavos. Some later editions read: fears, or complaints.

way is to face the enemy in the field, and not wait till he plunders us in our very[56] bedchamber.

Honeywood. Why, sir, as to the best, that—that's a very wise way too.

Mrs. Croaker. But can any thing be more absurd, than to double our distresses by our apprehensions, and put it in the power of every low fellow, that can scrawl ten words of wretched spelling, to torment us?

Honeywood. Without doubt, nothing more absurd.

Croaker. How! would it not be more absurd to despise the rattle till we are bit by the snake?

Honeywood. Without doubt, perfectly absurd.

Croaker. Then you are of my opinion?

Honeywood. Entirely.

Mrs. Croaker. And you reject mine?

Honeywood. Heaven forbid, madam! No, sure, no reasoning can be more just than yours. We ought certainly to despise malice, if we cannot oppose it, and not make the incendiary's pen as fatal to our repose as the highwayman's pistol.

Mrs. Croaker. O! then you think I'm quite right?

Honeywood. Perfectly right!

Croaker. A plague of plagues, we can't be both right. I ought to be sorry, or I ought to be glad. My hat must be on my head, or my hat must be off.[57]

Mrs. Croaker. Certainly, in two opposite opinions, if one be perfectly reasonable, the other can't be perfectly right.

Honeywood. And why may not both be right, madam? Mr. Croaker, in earnestly seeking redress, and you, in waiting the event with good humour? Pray let me see the letter again. I have it. This letter requires twenty guineas to be left at the bar of the Talbot inn. If it be indeed an incendiary letter, what if you and I, sir, go there; and, when the writer comes to be paid his expected booty, seize him?

Croaker. My dear friend, it's the very thing; the very thing. While I walk by the door, you shall plant yourself in ambush near the bar; burst out upon the miscreant like a masqued battery; extort a confession at once, and so hang him up by surprise.

---

[56] O1-O3, misprint, very very.

[57] This is perhaps modelled on *Il faut qu'une parte soit ouverte ou fermée*—quoted in *Citizen of the World*, 1762, i. Letter XLIX.

Honeywood. Yes; but I would not chuse to exercise too much severity. It is my maxim, sir, that crimes generally punish themselves.

Croaker [*Ironically*]. Well, but we may upbraid him a little, I suppose?

Honeywood. Ay, but not punish him too rigidly.

Croaker. Well, well, leave that to my own benevolence.

Honeywood. Well, I do; but remember that universal benevolence is the first law of nature.

[*Exeunt* HONEYWOOD *and* MRS. CROAKER.

Croaker. Yes; and my universal benevolence will hang the dog, if he had as many necks as a hydra!

ACT THE FIFTH

SCENE—*An Inn*

Enter OLIVIA, JARVIS.

OLIVIA. Well, we have got safe to the inn, however. Now, if the post-chaise were ready—

Jarvis. The horses are just finishing their oats; and, as they are not going to be married, they chuse to take their own time.

Olivia. You are for ever giving wrong motives to my impatience.

Jarvis. Be as impatient as you will, the horses must take their own time; besides, you don't consider, we have got no answer from our fellow traveller yet. If we hear nothing from Mr. Leontine, we have only one way left us.

Olivia. What way?

Jarvis. The way home again.

Olivia. Not so. I have made a resolution to go, and nothing shall induce me to break it.

Jarvis. Ay; resolutions are well kept when they jump with inclination. However, I'll go hasten things without. And I'll call, too, at the bar to see if any thing should be left for us there. Don't be in such a plaguy hurry, madam, and we shall go the faster, I promise you.   [*Exit* JARVIS.

Enter LANDLADY.

Landlady. What, Solomon! why don't you move? Pipes

and tobacco for the Lamb there.[58]—Will nobody answer? To the Dolphin; quick. The Angel has been outrageous this half hour. Did your ladyship call, madam?

Olivia. No, madam.

Landlady. I find as you're for Scotland, madam—But that's no business of mine; married, or not married, I ask no questions. To be sure, we had a sweet little couple set off from this two days ago for the same place. The gentleman, for a taylor, was, to be sure, as fine a spoken taylor as ever blew froth from a full pot. And the young lady so bashful, it was near half an hour before we could get her to finish a pint of rasberry between us.

Olivia. But this gentleman and I are not going to be married, I assure you.

Landlady. May be not. That's no business of mine; for certain, Scotch marriages seldom turn out well.[59] There was, of my own knowledge, Miss Macfag, that married her father's footman.—Alack-a-day, she and her husband soon parted, and now keep separate cellars[60] in Hedge-Lane.[61]

Olivia [*Aside*]. A very pretty picture of what lies before me.

Enter LEONTINE.

Leontine. My dear Olivia, my anxiety till you were out of danger was too great to be resisted. I could not help coming to see you set out, tho' it exposes us to a discovery.

Olivia. May every thing you do prove as fortunate. Indeed, Leontine, we have been most cruelly disappointed. Mr. Honeywood's bill upon the city has, it seems, been protested, and we have been utterly at a loss how to proceed.

Leontine. How! An offer of his own too! Sure, he could not mean to deceive us.

Olivia. Depend upon his sincerity; he only mistook the

---

[58] In the eighteenth century, the rooms of inns had generally names in lieu of numbers.

[59] *Turn out well.* Octavos to O5 omit well.

[60] Goldsmith repeats this idea in his essay on Scotch Marriages. See p. 106, l. 27.

[61] Hedge-Lane now Dorset Street, leads from Pall Mall east to Coventry Street, Haymarket.

desire for the power of serving us. But let us think no more of it. I believe the post-chaise is ready by this.

Landlady. Not quite yet: and, begging your ladyship's pardon, I don't think your ladyship quite ready for the post-chaise. The North Road is a cold place, madam. I have a drop in the house of as pretty rasberry as ever was tipt over tongue. Just a thimblefull to keep the wind off your stomach. To be sure, the last couple we had here, they said it was a perfect nosegay. Ecod, I sent them both away as good natur'd— Up went the blinds, round went the wheels, and drive away post-boy was the word.

Enter CROAKER.

Croaker. Well, while my friend Honeywood is upon the post of danger at the bar, it must be my business to have an eye about me here. I think I know an incendiary's look; for, wherever the devil makes a purchase, he never fails to set his mark. Ha! who have we here? My son and daughter! What can they be doing here?

Landlady. I tell you, madam, it will do you good; I think I know by this time what's good for the North Road. It's a raw night, madam—sir—

Leontine. Not a drop more, good madam. I should now take it as a greater favour, if you hasten the horses, for I am afraid to be seen myself.

Landlady. That shall be done. Wha, Solomon! are you all dead there? Wha, Solomon, I say!   [*Exit bawling.*

Olivia. Well; I dread lest an expedition begun in fear should end in repentance.—Every moment we stay increases our danger, and adds to my apprehensions.

Leontine. There's no danger, trust me, my dear; there can be none: if Honeywood has acted with honour, and kept my father, as he promised, in employment till we are out of danger, nothing can interrupt our journey.

Olivia. I have no doubt of Mr. Honeywood's sincerity, and even his desires to serve us. My fears are from your father's suspicions. A mind so disposed to be alarmed without a cause, will be but too ready when there's a reason.

Leontine. Why, let him, when we are out of his power. But, believe me, Olivia, you have no great reason to dread his resentment. His repining temper, as it does no manner of injury to himself, so will it never do harm to others. He only frets to keep himself employed, and scolds for his private amusement.

Olivia. I don't know that; but, I'm sure, on some occasions, it makes him look most shockingly.

Croaker [*Discovering himself*]. How does he look now? —How does he look now?

Olivia. Ah!

Leontine. Undone.

Croaker. How do I look now? Sir, I am your very humble servant. Madam, I am your's. What, you are going off, are you? Then, first, if you please, take a word or two from me with you before you go. Tell me first where you are going, and when you have told me that, perhaps I shall know as little as I did before.

Leontine. If that be so, our answer might but increase your displeasure, without adding to your information.

Croaker. I want no information from you, puppy: and you, too, good madam, what answer have you got? Eh! [*A cry without,* "*Stop him.*"] I think I heard a noise. My friend Honeywood without—has he seized the incendiary? Ah, no, for now I hear no more on't.

Leontine. Honeywood, without! Then, sir, it was Mr. Honeywood that directed you hither.[62]

Croaker. No, sir, it was Mr. Honeywood conducted me hither.

Leontine. Is it possible?

Croaker. Possible! Why, he's in the house now, sir. More anxious about me than my own son, sir.

Leontine. Then, sir, he's a villain!

Croaker. How, sirrah! a villain, because he takes most care of your father? I'll not bear it. I tell you I'll not bear it. Honeywood is a friend to the family, and I'll have him treated as such.

Leontine. I shall study to repay his friendship as it deserves.

Croaker. Ah rogue, if you knew how earnestly he entered into my griefs and pointed out the means to detect them, you would love him as I do. [*A cry without,* "*Stop him.*"] Fire and fury! they have seized the incendiary: they have the villain, the incendiary, in view. Stop him, stop an incendiary, a murderer; stop him!   [*Exit.*

Olivia. Oh, my terrors! What can this new tumult mean?

Leontine. Some new mark, I suppose, of Mr. Honey-

[62] O1, hither? Other octavos, period.

wood's sincerity. But we shall have satisfaction: he shall give me instant satisfaction.

Olivia. It must not be, my Leontine, if you value my esteem, or my happiness. Whatever be our fate, let us not add guilt to our misfortunes— Consider that our innocence will shortly be all we have left us. You must forgive him.

Leontine. Forgive him! Has he not in every instance betrayed us? Forced me to borrow money from him, which appears a mere trick to delay us: promised to keep my father engaged till we were out of danger, and here brought him to the very scene of our escape?

Olivia. Don't be precipitate. We may yet be mistaken.

Enter POSTBOY, *dragging in* JARVIS: HONEYWOOD *entering soon after.*

Postboy. Ay, master, we have him fast enough. Here is the incendiary dog. I'm entitled to the reward; I'll take my oath I saw him ask for the money at the bar, and then run for it.

Honeywood. Come, bring him along. Let us see him! Let him learn to blush for his crimes. [*Discovering his mistake.*] Death! what's here? Jarvis, Leontine, Olivia! What can all this mean?

Jarvis. Why, I'll tell you what it means: that I was an old fool, and that you are my master—that's all.

Honeywood. Confusion!

Leontine. Yes, sir, I find you have kept your word with me. After such baseness, I wonder how you can venture to see the man you have injured.

Honeywood. My dear Leontine, by my life, my honour—

Leontine. Peace, peace, for shame; and do not continue to aggravate baseness by hypocrisy. I know you, sir, I know you.

Honeywood. Why, won't you hear me! By all that's just, I knew not—

Leontine. Hear you, sir! to what purpose? I now see through all your low arts; your ever complying with every opinion; your never refusing any request; your friendship as common as a prostitute's favours, and as fallacious; all these, sir, have long been contemptible to the world, and are now perfectly so to me.

Honeywood [*Aside*]. Ha! "Contemptible to the world"! That reaches me.

Leontine. All the seeming sincerity of your professions I now find were only allurements to betray; and all your seeming regret for their consequences only calculated to cover the cowardice of your heart. Draw, villain!

Enter CROAKER, *out of breath.*

Croaker. Where is the villain? Where is the incendiary? [*Seizing the* POSTBOY.] Hold him fast, the dog; he has the gallows in his face. Come, you dog, confess; confess all, and hang yourself.

Postboy. Zounds, master! what do you throttle me for?

Croaker [*Beating him*]. Dog, do you resist; do you resist?

Postboy. Zounds, master! I'm not he; there's the man that we thought was the rogue, and turns out to be one of the company.

Croaker. How!

Honeywood. Mr. Croaker, we have all been under a strange mistake here; I find there is nobody guilty; it was all an error; entirely an error of our own.

Croaker. And I say, sir, that you're in an error; for there's guilt and double guilt, a plot, a damn'd Jesuitical, pestilential plot; and I must have proof of it.

Honeywood. Do but hear me.

Croaker. What, you intend to bring 'em off, I suppose; I'll hear nothing.

Honeywood. Madam, you seem at least calm enough to hear reason.

Olivia. Excuse me.

Honeywood. Good Jarvis, let me then explain it to you.

Jarvis. What signifies explanation when the thing is done?

Honeywood. Will nobody hear me? Was there ever such a set, so blinded by passion and prejudice! [*To the* POSTBOY.] My good friend, I believe you'll be surprised when I assure you—

Postboy. Sure me nothing—I'm sure of nothing but a good beating.

Croaker. Come then, you, madam, if you ever hope for any favour or forgiveness, tell me sincerely all you know of this affair.

Olivia. Unhappily, sir, I'm but too much the cause of your suspicions: you see before you, sir, one that with false pretences has stept into your family to betray it: not your daughter—

Croaker. Not my daughter!

Olivia. Not your daughter—but a mean deceiver—who —support me, I cannot—

Honeywood. Help, she's going, give her air.

Croaker. Ay, ay, take the young woman to the air; I would not hurt a hair of her head, whose ever daughter she may be—not so bad as that neither.

[*Exeunt all but* CROAKER.

Croaker. Yes, yes, all's out; I now see the whole affair: my son is neither married, or going to be so, to this lady, whom he imposed upon me as his sister. Ay, certainly so; and yet I don't find it afflicts me so much as one might think. There's the advantage of fretting away our misfortunes beforehand, we never feel them when they come.

Enter MISS RICHLAND *and* SIR WILLIAM.

Sir William. But how do you know, madam, that my nephew intends setting off from this place?

Miss Richland. My maid assured me he was come to this inn, and my own knowledge of his intending to leave the kingdom suggested the rest. But what do I see, my guardian here before us! Who, my dear sir, could have expected meeting you here; to what accident do we owe this pleasure?

Croaker. To a fool, I believe.

Miss Richland. But to what purpose did you come?

Croaker. To play the fool.

Miss Richland. But with whom?

Croaker. With greater fools than myself.

Miss Richland. Explain.

Croaker. Why, Mr. Honeywood brought me here, to do nothing now I am here; and my son is going to be married to I don't know who that is here; so now you are as wise as I am.

Miss Richland. Married! to whom, sir?

Croaker. To Olivia; my daughter, as I took her to be; but who the devil she is, or whose daughter she is, I know no more than the man in the moon.

Sir William. Then, sir, I can inform you; and, tho' a stranger, yet you shall find me a friend to your family: it will be enough, at present, to assure you that, both in point of birth and fortune, the young lady is at least your son's equal. Being left by her father, Sir James Wood-ville—

Croaker. Sir James Woodville! What, of the West?

Sir William. Being left by him, I say, to the care of a mercenary wretch, whose only aim was to secure her fortune to himself, she was sent into France, under pretence of education; and there every art was tried to fix her for life in a convent, contrary to her inclinations. Of this I was informed upon my arrival at Paris; and, as I had been once her father's friend, I did all in my power to frustrate her guardian's base intentions. I had even meditated to rescue her from his authority, when your son stept in with more pleasing violence, gave her liberty, and you a daughter.

Croaker. But I intend to have a daughter of my own chusing, sir. A young lady, sir, whose fortune, by my interest with those that have interest, will be double what my son has a right to expect! Do you know Mr. Lofty, sir?

Sir William. Yes, sir; and know that you are deceived in him. But step this way, and I'll convince you.

CROAKER *and* SIR WILLIAM *seem to confer.*
Enter HONEYWOOD.

Honeywood. Obstinate man, still to persist in his outrage! Insulted by him, despis'd by all, I now begin to grow contemptible, even to myself. How have I sunk by too great an assiduity to please! How have I overtax'd all my abilities, lest the approbation of a single fool should escape me! But all is now over; I have survived my reputation, my fortune, my friendships, and nothing remains henceforward for me but solitude and repentance.

Miss Richland. Is it true, Mr. Honeywood, that you are setting off without taking leave of your friends? The report is that you are quitting England. Can it be?

Honeywood. Yes, madam; and tho' I am so unhappy as to have fallen under your displeasure, yet, thank Heaven, I leave you to happiness; to one who loves you, and deserves your love; to one who has power to produce you affluence, and generosity to improve your enjoyment of it.

Miss Richland. And are you sure, sir, that the gentleman you mean is what you describe him?

Honeywood. I have the best assurances of it, his serving

me. He does indeed deserve the highest happiness, and
that is in your power to confer. As for me, weak and
wavering as I have been, obliged by all, and incapable
of serving any, what happiness can I find but in solitude;
what hope but in being forgotten?

Miss Richland. A thousand! to live among friends that
esteem you, whose happiness it will be to be permitted to
oblige you.

Honeywood. No, madam; my resolution is fix'd. In-
feriority among strangers is easy; but among those that
once were equals, insupportable. Nay, to shew you how
far my resolution can go, I can now speak with calmness
of my former follies, my vanity, my dissipation, my weakness. I will even confess that, among the number of my
other presumptions, I had the insolence to think of loving
you. Yes, madam, while I was pleading the passion of another, my heart was tortur'd with its own.[63] But it is over,
it was unworthy our friendship, and let it be forgotten.

Miss Richland. You amaze me!

Honeywood. But you'll forgive it, I know you will; since
the confession should not have come from me even now
but to convince you of the sincerity of my intention of—
never mentioning it more.   [*Going.*

Miss Richland. Stay, sir, one moment—Ha! he here—

Enter LOFTY.

Lofty. Is the coast clear? None but friends. I have fol-
lowed you here with a trifling piece of intelligence: but
it goes no farther, things are not yet ripe for a discovery.
I have spirits working at a certain board; your affair at the
Treasury will be done in less than—a thousand years.
Mum!

Miss Richland. Sooner, sir, I should hope!

Lofty. Why, yes, I believe it may, if it falls into proper
hands, that know where to push and where to parry; that
know how the land lies—eh, Honeywood?

Miss Richland. It is fallen into yours.

Lofty. Well, to keep you no longer in suspense, your
thing is done. It is done, I say—that's all. I have just had
assurances from Lord Neverout that the claim has been
examined, and found admissible. *Quietus* is the word,
madam.

[63] This, it may be remarked, is precisely the case of
M. Rostand's *Cyrano de Bergerac.*

Honeywood. But how! his Lordship has been at New-market these ten days!

Lofty. Indeed! Then Sir Gilbert Goose must have been most damnably mistaken. I had it of him.

Miss Richland. He! why, Sir Gilbert and his family have been in the country this month!

Lofty. This month! It must certainly be so—Sir Gilbert's letter did come to me from Newmarket, so that he must have met his Lordship there; and so it came about. I have his letter about me; I'll read it to you. [*Taking out a large bundle.*] That's from Paoli of Corsica,[64] that from the Marquis of Squilachi.[65]—Have you a mind to see a letter from Count Poniatowski,[66] now King of Poland—Honest Pon—[*Searching.*] O, sir, what, are you here too? I'll tell you what, honest friend, if you have not absolutely delivered my letter to Sir William Honeywood, you may return it. The thing will do without him.

Sir William. Sir, I have delivered it, and must inform you it was received with the most mortifying contempt.

Croaker. Contempt! Mr. Lofty, what can that mean?

Lofty. Let him go on, let him go on, I say. You'll find it come to something presently.

Sir William. Yes, sir, I believe you'll be amazed, if, after waiting some time in the anti-chamber, after being surveyed with insolent curiosity by the passing servants, I was at last assured that Sir William Honeywood knew no such person and I must certainly have been imposed upon.[67]

Lofty. Good; let me die, very good. Ha! ha! ha!

Croaker. Now, for my life, I can't find out half the goodness of it.

Lofty. You can't? Ha! ha!

Croaker. No, for the soul of me; I think it was as confounded a bad answer as ever was sent from one private gentleman to another.

Lofty. And so you can't find out the force of the message? Why, I was in the house at that very time. Ha! ha!

[64] Pascal Paoli (1726-1807) was a Corsican patriot, at this time in London.

[65] Squilachi (Squillaci) was Prime Minister at Madrid.

[66] Stanislaus-Augustus Poniatowski, last king of Poland, 1732-98.

[67] Sir William Honeywood is here competing with Lofty—in romance.

It was I that sent that very answer to my own letter.
Ha! ha!

Croaker. Indeed! How! why!

Lofty. In one word, things between Sir William and
me must be behind the curtain. A party has many eyes.
He sides with Lord Buzzard, I side with Sir Gilbert
Goose. So that unriddles the mystery.

Croaker. And so it does indeed, and all my suspicions
are over.

Lofty. Your suspicions! What then, you have been suspecting, you have been suspecting, have you? Mr. Croaker,
you and I were friends, we are friends no longer. Never
talk to me. It's over; I say, it's over!

Croaker. As I hope for your favour, I did not mean to
offend. It escaped me. Don't be discomposed.

Lofty. Zounds, sir, but I am discomposed, and will be
discomposed. To be treated thus! Who am I? Was it for
this I have been dreaded both by ins and outs? Have I
been libelled in the *Gazetteer*,[68] and praised in the *St.
James's*;[69] have I been chaired at Wildman's,[70] and a
speaker at Merchant Taylor's Hall;[71] have I had my hand
to addresses, and my head in the print-shops, and talk to
me of suspects?

Croaker. My dear sir, be pacified. What can you have
but asking pardon?

Lofty. Sir, I will not be pacified—Suspects! Who am I?
To be used thus, have I paid court to men in favour to
serve my friends, the Lords of the Treasury, Sir William
Honeywood, and the rest of the gang, and talk to me of
suspects! Who am I, I say, who am I?

Sir William. Since, sir, you're so pressing for an answer,
I'll tell you who you are. A gentleman as well acquainted
with politics as with men in power; as well acquainted
with persons of fashion as with modesty; with Lords of the

[68] A well-known and rather unscrupulous daily, printed for
a short period by Samuel Richardson.

[69] The *St. James's Chronicle*.

[70] A coffee-house in Bedford Street, Strand, the favourite
headquarters of the supporters of John Wilkes. "Each dish at
WILDMAN's of Sedition smacks." Churchill, *The Candidate*
(*Poems*, 1769, ii. 202). Horace Walpole also mentions it in a
letter to Lord Hertford, 9 Nov., 1764.

[71] Merchant Taylors' Hall, in Threadneedle Street, is still
famous for its banquets.

Treasury as with truth; and with all as you are with Sir
William Honeywood. I am Sir William Honeywood!

[*Discovering his ensigns of the Bath.*

Croaker. Sir William Honeywood!

Honeywood [*Aside*]. Astonishment! my uncle!

Lofty. So, then, my confounded genius has been all this
time only leading me up to the garret in order to fling me
out of the window.

Croaker. What, Mr. Importance, and are these your
works? Suspect you! You who have been dreaded by the
ins and outs: you who have had your hand to addresses,
and your head stuck up in print-shops. If you were served
right, you should have your head stuck up in the pillory.

Lofty. Ay, stick it where you will, for, by the Lord, it
cuts but a very poor figure where it sticks at present.

Sir William. Well, Mr. Croaker, I hope you now see
how incapable this gentleman is of serving you, and how
little Miss Richland has to expect from his influence.

Croaker. Ay, sir, too well I see it, and I can't but say
I have had some boding of it these ten days. So I'm resolved, since my son has placed his affections on a lady of
moderate fortune, to be satisfied with his choice, and not
run the hazard of another Mr. Lofty, in helping him to
a better.

Sir William. I approve your resolution; and here they
come, to receive a confirmation of your pardon and consent.

Enter MRS. CROAKER, JARVIS, LEONTINE, OLIVIA.

Mrs. Croaker. Where's my husband? Come, come,
lovey, you must forgive them. Jarvis here has been to tell
me the whole affair; and I say you must forgive them.
Our own was a stolen match, you know, my dear; and
we never had any reason to repent of it.

Croaker. I wish we could both say so: however, this
gentleman, Sir William Honeywood, has been beforehand
with you in obtaining their pardon. So, if the two poor
fools have a mind to marry, I think we can tack them
together without crossing the Tweed for it.

[*Joining their hands.*

Leontine. How blest and unexpected! What, what can
we say to such goodness! But our future obedience shall be
the best reply. And, as for this gentleman, to whom we
owe—

Sir William. Excuse me, sir, if I interrupt your thanks, as I have here an interest that calls me. [*Turning to* HONEYWOOD.] Yes, sir, you are surprised to see me; and I own that a desire of correcting your follies led me hither. I saw with indignation the errors of a mind that only sought applause from others; that easiness of disposition which, tho' inclin'd to the right, had not courage to condemn the wrong. I saw with regret those splendid errors that still took name from some neighbouring duty. Your charity that was but injustice; your benevolence that was but weakness; and your friendship but credulity. I saw with regret great talents and extensive learning only employed to add sprightliness to error and encrease your perplexities. I saw your mind with a thousand natural charms; but the greatness of its beauty served only to heighten my pity for its prostitution.

Honeywood. Cease to upbraid me, sir; I have for some time but too strongly felt the justice of your reproaches. But there is one way still left me. Yes, sir, I have determined this very hour to quit forever a place where I have made myself the voluntary slave of all; and to seek among strangers that fortitude which may give strength to the mind and marshal all its dissipated virtues. Yet, ere I depart, permit me to solicit favour for this gentleman, who, notwithstanding what has happened, has laid me under the most signal obligations. Mr. Lofty—

Lofty. Mr. Honeywood, I'm resolv'd upon a reformation as well as you. I now begin to find that the man who first invented the art of speaking truth was a much cunninger fellow than I thought him. And to prove that I design to speak truth for the future, I must now assure you that you owe your late enlargement to another, as, upon my soul, I had no hand in the matter. So now, if any of the company has a mind for preferment, he may take my place. I'm determined to resign.   [*Exit.*

Honeywood. How have I been deceived!

Sir William. No sir, you have been obliged to a kinder, fairer friend for that favour. To Miss Richland. Would she complete our joy, and make the man she has honoured by her friendship happy in her love, I should then forget all, and be as blest as the welfare of my dearest kinsman can make me.

Miss Richland. After what is past, it would be but affectation to pretend to indifference. Yes, I will own an attachment which, I find, was more than friendship. And if my intreaties cannot alter his resolution to quit the country, I will even try if my hand has not power to detain him.   [*Giving her hand.*

Honeywood. Heavens! how can I have deserved all this? How express my happiness, my gratitude? A moment like this over-pays an age of apprehension!

Croaker. Well, now I see content in every face; but Heaven send we be all better this day three months.

Sir William. Henceforth, nephew, learn to respect yourself. He who seeks only for applause from without, has all his happiness in another's keeping.

Honeywood. Yes, sir, I now too plainly perceive my errors. My vanity, in attempting to please all by fearing to offend any. My meanness, in approving folly lest fools should disapprove. Henceforth, therefore, it shall be my study to reserve my pity for real distress; my friendship for true merit, and my love for her who first taught me what it is to be happy.

EPILOGUE [72]

Spoken by Mrs. Bulkley [73]

As puffing quacks some caitiff wretch procure
To swear the pill, or drop, has wrought a cure;
Thus, on the stage, our playwrights still depend
For Epilogues and Prologues on some friend,
Who knows each art of coaxing up the town,
And makes[74] full many a bitter pill go down.
Conscious of this, our bard has gone about,
And teaz'd each rhyming friend to help him out.
An Epilogue, things can't go on without it,
It could not fail, wou'd you but set about it.

[72] The Author in expectation of an epilogue from a friend at Oxford deferred writing one himself till the very last hour. What is here offered owes all its success to the graceful manner of the Actress who spoke it.

[73] Mrs. Bulkley, formerly Miss Wilford. She subsequently acted Miss Hardcastle in *She Stoops to Conquer*.

[74] *makes.* Make in octavos.

Young man, cries one (a bard laid up in clover),
Alas, young man, my writing days are over;
Let boys play tricks, and kick the straw,[75] not I;
Your brother Doctor[76] there, perhaps, may try.
What I, dear sir, the Doctor interposes,
What, plant my thistle, sir, among his roses!
No, no, I've other contests to maintain;
To-night I head our troops at Warwick-Lane.[77]
Go, ask your manager[78]—Who, me?[79] Your pardon;
Those things are not our fort at Covent-Garden.
Our Author's friends, thus plac'd at happy distance,
Give him good words indeed, but no assistance.
As some unhappy wight, at some new play,
At the Pit door stands elbowing away,
While oft, with many a smile, and many a shrug,
He eyes the centre, where his friends sit snug,
His simpering friends, with pleasure in their eyes,
Sink as he sinks, and as he rises rise:
He nods, they nod; he cringes, they grimace;
But not a soul will budge to give him place.
Since then, unhelp'd, our bard must now conform
To 'bide the pelting[80] of this pittiless storm,
Blame where you must, be candid where you can,
And be each critick[81] the Good-natur'd Man.

[75] To play a trivial game.

[76] Your brother Doctor. Goldsmith was a doctor; but which of his brethren is here referred to has not been revealed.

[77] Wren's old College of Physicians—at this date in hot dispute with respect to the exclusion of certain Licentiates from Fellowships—stood on the west side of Warwick Lane, which runs between Newgate Street and Paternoster Row.

[78] The elder Colman, then one of the patentees of Covent Garden Theatre.

[79] *Who, me?* O1, O2 Who, me!

[80] *King Lear*, Act III. Sc. 4.

[81] *And be each critick*. O1 and O2 read: And view with favour.

AN ESSAY ON THE THEATRE

AN ESSAY ON THE THEATRE; OR, A COMPARISON BETWEEN LAUGHING AND SENTIMENTAL COMEDY.[1]

THE THEATRE, like all other amusements, has its fashions and its prejudices: and when satiated with its excellence, mankind begin to mistake change for improvement. For some years tragedy was the reigning entertainment; but of late it has entirely given way to comedy, and our best efforts are now exerted in these lighter kinds of composition. The pompous train, the swelling phrase, and the unnatural rant, are displaced for that natural portrait of human folly and frailty, of which all are judges, because all have sat for the picture.

But as in describing nature it is presented with a double face, either of mirth or sadness, our modern writers find themselves at a loss which chiefly to copy from; and it is now debated, whether the exhibition of human distress is likely to afford the mind more entertainment than that of human absurdity?

Comedy is defined by Aristotle to be a picture of the frailties of the lower part of mankind, to distinguish it from tragedy, which is an exhibition of the misfortunes of the great. When comedy, therefore, ascends to produce the characters of princes or generals upon the stage, it is out of its walks, since low life and middle life are entirely its object. The principal question, therefore, is, whether, in describing low or middle life, an exhibition of its follies be not preferable to a detail of its calamities? Or, in other words, which deserves the preference,—the weeping sentimental comedy so much in fashion at present, or the laughing, and even low comedy, which seems to have been last exhibited by Vanbrugh and Cibber?

If we apply to authorities, all the great masters in the dramatic art have but one opinion. Their rule is, that as tragedy displays the calamities of the great, so comedy should excite our laughter by ridiculously exhibiting the follies of the lower part of mankind. Boileau, one of the best modern critics, asserts, that comedy will not admit of tragic distress:—

[1] This was contributed by Goldsmith to the *Westminster Magazine* (Vol. i. p. 4).

"Le comique, ennemi des soupirs et des pleurs,
   N'admet point dans ses vers de tragiques douleurs." [2]

Nor is this rule without the strongest foundation in nature, as the distresses of the mean by no means affect us so
strongly as the calamities of the great. When tragedy ex-
hibits to us some great man fallen from his height, and
struggling with want and adversity, we feel his situation
in the same manner as we suppose he himself must feel,
and our pity is increased in proportion to the height from
which he fell. On the contrary, we do not so strongly
sympathise with one born in humbler circumstances, and
encountering accidental distress: so that while we melt
for Belisarius, we scarcely give halfpence to the beggar
who accosts us in the street. The one has our pity; the
other our contempt. Distress, therefore, is the proper object of tragedy, since the great excite our pity by their
fall; but not equally so of comedy, since the actors employed in it are originally so mean, that they sink but
little by their fall.

Since the first origin of the stage, tragedy and comedy
have run in distinct channels, and never till of late encroached upon the provinces of each other. Terence, who
seems to have made the nearest approaches, always ju-
diciously stops short before he comes to the downright
pathetic; and yet he is even reproached by Cæsar for
wanting the *vis comica*. All the other comic writers of
antiquity aim only at rendering folly or vice ridiculous,
but never exalt their characters into buskined pomp, or
make what Voltaire humorously calls *a tradesman's
tragedy*.

Yet notwithstanding this weight of authority, and the
universal practice of former ages, a new species of dramatic composition has been introduced, under the name
of *sentimental* comedy, in which the virtues of private
life are exhibited, rather than the vices exposed; and the
distresses rather than the faults of mankind make our interest in the piece. These comedies have had of late great
success, perhaps from their novelty, and also from their
flattering every man in his favourable foible. In these plays
almost all the characters are good, and exceedingly generous; they are lavish enough of their *tin* money on the
stage; and though they want humour, have abundance of

    [2] *L'Art Poetique,* chant iii.

sentiment and feeling. If they happen to have faults or foibles, the spectator is taught, not only to pardon, but to applaud them, in consideration of the goodness of their hearts; so that folly, instead of being ridiculed, is commended, and the comedy aims at touching our passions without the power of being truly pathetic. In this manner we are likely to lose one great source of entertainment on the stage; for while the comic poet is invading the province of the tragic muse, he leaves her lovely sister quite neglected. Of this, however, he is no way solicitous, as he measures his fame by his profits.

But it will be said, that the theatre is formed to amuse mankind, and that it matters little, if this end be answered, by what means it is obtained. If mankind find delight in weeping at comedy, it would be cruel to abridge them in that or any other innocent pleasure. If those pieces are denied the name of comedies, yet call them by any other name and, if they are delightful, they are good. Their success, it will be said, is a mark of their merit, and it is only abridging our happiness to deny us an inlet to amusement.

These objections, however, are rather specious than solid. It is true, that amusement is a great object of the theatre, and it will be allowed that these sentimental pieces do often amuse us; but the question is, whether the true comedy would not amuse us more? The question is, whether a character supported throughout a piece, with its ridicule still attending, would not give us more delight than this species of bastard tragedy, which only is applauded because it is new?

A friend of mine, who was sitting unmoved at one of these sentimental pieces, was asked how he could be so indifferent? "Why, truly," says he, "as the hero is but a tradesman, it is indifferent to me whether he be turned out of his counting-house on Fish Street Hill, since he will still have enough left to open shop in St. Giles's."

The other objection is as ill-grounded; for though we should give these pieces another name, it will not mend their efficacy. It will continue a kind of *mulish* production, with all the defects of its opposite parents, and marked with sterility. If we are permitted to make comedy weep, we have an equal right to make tragedy laugh, and to set down in blank verse the jests and repartees of all the attendants in a funeral procession.

But there is one argument in favour of sentimental comedy, which will keep it on the stage, in spite of all that can be said against it. It is, of all others, the most easily written. Those abilities that can hammer out a novel are fully sufficient for the production of a sentimental comedy. It is only sufficient to raise the characters a little; to deck out the hero with a riband, or give the heroine a title; then to put an insipid dialogue, without character or humour, into their mouths, give them mighty good hearts, very fine clothes, furnish a new set of scenes, make a pathetic scene or two, with a sprinkling of tender melancholy conversation through the whole, and there is no doubt but all the ladies will cry, and all the gentlemen applaud.

Humour at present seems to be departing from the stage, and it will soon happen that our comic players will have nothing left for it but a fine coat and a song. It depends upon the audience whether they will actually drive those poor merry creatures from the stage, or sit at a play as gloomy as at the Tabernacle.[3] It is not easy to recover an art when once lost; and it will be but a just punishment, that when, by our being too fastidious, we have banished humour from the stage, we should ourselves be deprived of the art of laughing.

[3] Whitefield's Tabernacle in Tottenham Court Road.

A REGISTER OF SCOTCH MARRIAGES

A REGISTER OF SCOTCH MARRIAGES

To the Editor of "The Westminster Magazine." [1]

SIR,—As I see you are fond of gallantry, and seem willing to set young people together as soon as you can, I cannot help lending my assistance to your endeavours, as I am greatly concerned in the attempt. You must know, sir, that I am landlady of one of the most noted inns on the road to Scotland, and have seldom less than eight or ten couples a week, who go down rapturous lovers, and return man and wife.

If there be in this world an agreeable situation, it must be that in which a young couple find themselves when just let loose from confinement, and whirling off to the land of promise. When the post-chaise is driving off, and the blinds are drawn up, sure nothing can equal it! And yet, I do not know how, what with the fears of being pursued, or the wishes for greater happiness, not one of my customers but seems gloomy and out of temper. The gentlemen are all sullen, and the ladies discontented.

But if it be so going down, how is it with them coming back? Having been for a fortnight together, they are then mighty good company to be sure. It is then the young lady's indiscretion stares her in the face; and the gentleman himself finds that much is to be done before the money comes in.

For my own part, sir, I was married in the usual way; all my friends were at the wedding; I was conducted with great ceremony from the table to the bed: and I do not find that it any ways diminished my happiness with my husband, while, poor man, he continued with me. For my part, I am entirely for doing things in the old family way; I hate your new-fashioned manners, and never loved an outlandish marriage in my life.

As I have had numbers call at my house, you may be sure I was not idle in inquiring who they were, and how they did in the world after they left me. I cannot say that I ever heard much good come of them; and of a history of twenty-five that I noted down in my ledger, I do not

[1] This letter, by Goldsmith, appeared in the *Westminster Magazine* for February, 1773 (vol. i. p. 173). See *Good Natur'd Man*, pp. 82-84.

know a single couple that would not have been full as happy if they had gone the plain way to work, and asked the consent of their parents. To convince you of it, I will mention the names of a few, and refer the rest to some fitter opportunity.

Imprimis, Miss Jenny Hastings went down to Scotland with a tailor, who, to be sure, for a tailor, was a very agreeable sort of a man. But I do not know how, he did not take proper measure of the young lady's disposition: they quarrelled at my house on their return; so she left him for a cornet of dragoons, and he went back to his shopboard.

Miss Rachel Runfort went off with a grenadier. They spent all their money going down; so that he carried her down in a post-chaise, and, coming back, she helped to carry his knapsack.

Miss Racket went down with her lover in their own phaeton; but upon their return, being very fond of driving, she would be every now and then for holding the whip. This bred a dispute; and before they were a fortnight together, she felt that he could exercise the whip on somebody else besides the horses.

Miss Meekly, though all compliance to the will of her lover, could never reconcile him to the change of his situation. It seems, he married her supposing she had a large fortune; but being deceived in their expectations, they parted; and they now keep separate garrets in Rosemary Lane.[2]

The next couple of whom I have any account, actually lived together in great harmony and uncloying kindness for no less than a month; but the lady, who was a little in years, having parted with her fortune to her dearest life, he left her to make love to that better part of her which he valued more.

The next pair consisted of an Irish fortune-hunter and one of the prettiest, modestest ladies that ever my eyes beheld. As he was a well-looking gentleman, all drest in lace, and as she seemed very fond of him, I thought they were blest for life. Yet I was quickly mistaken. The lady

[2] Rosemary Lane, or Rag Fair, now Royal Mint Street, Whitechapel, is a haunt of dealers in old clothes. Goldsmith also mentions it in his *Adventures of a Strolling Player* (*Essays*, 1765, xxi). Cf. *Good Natur'd Man*, Act v. (at beginning) as to "separate cellars in Hedge-Lane."

was no better than a common woman of the town, and he was no better than a sharper; so they agreed upon a mutual divorce. He now dresses at the York Ball,[3] and she is in keeping by the member for our borough in Parliament.

In this manner we see that all those marriages, in which there is interest on one side, and disobedience on the other, are not likely to promise a long harvest of delights. If our fortune-hunting gentlemen would but speak out, the young lady, instead of a lover, would often find a sneaking rogue, that only wanted the lady's purse, and not her heart. For my own part, I never saw anything but design and falsehood in every one of them; and my blood has boiled in my veins, when I saw a young fellow of twenty kneeling at the feet of a twenty thousand pounder, professing his passion, while he was taking aim at her money. I do not deny but there may be love in a Scotch marriage, but it is generally all on one side.

Of all the sincere admirers I ever knew, a man of my acquaintance, who, however, did not run away with his mistress to Scotland, was the most so. An old exciseman of our town, who, as you may guess, was not very rich, had a daughter who, as you shall see, was not very handsome. It was the opinion of everybody that this young woman would not soon be married, as she wanted two main articles, beauty and fortune. But for all this, a very well-looking man, that happened to be travelling those parts, came and asked the exciseman for his daughter in marriage. The exciseman, willing to deal openly by him, asked if he had seen the girl; "for," says he, "she is hump-backed." —"Very well," cried the stranger, "that will do for me."— "Aye," says the exciseman, "but my daughter is as brown as a berry."—"So much the better," cried the stranger, "such skins wear well." "But she is bandy-legged," says the exciseman.—"No matter," cries the other, "her petticoats will hide that defect."—"But then she is very poor, and wants an eye."—"Your description delights me," cries the stranger: "I have been looking out for one of her make; for I keep an exhibition of wild beasts, and intend to show her off for a Chimpanzee."

[3] Attends the Ball in search of dupes.

SHE STOOPS TO CONQUER:

OR,

THE MISTAKES OF A NIGHT

A COMEDY

THIS text of *She Stoops to Conquer* follows a copy, in the Library of Harvard College, of the fifth edition, the last published during Goldsmith's life. It has been collated, also, with copies of the first edition, a probable second from Mr. Robert Hoe's library, and a third in the Library of Columbia University. The first octavo, though it is not so marked, is easily recognized because its last page is numbered 114, an error originating in a pagination between signatures L2 *recto* and N *recto* which jumps backward and forward wildly, and results in assigning to the edition eight more pages than it really has. At the foot of the title-page are the words: "Price 1/6." It is often said that there are two forms of O1: the second has a half-title to which the price has been transferred, corrects the errors in pagination and signatures of O1, and prints the Cradock epilogue at the end of the play instead of just before the Dramatis Personæ. The collator suspects, however, that closer examination of this second form will show that it is really a second edition, for the edition called second here has all the characteristics of the so-called second form of O1, except the half-title,—which is often missing in editions otherwise perfect,—yet shows enough typographical differences from O1 to warrant calling it a different edition. The fact that it, like O1, prints the song of Tony at the end of the second act as part of his speech, corrected in O3, again suggests that it is O2. The third and the fifth editions bear the number on the title-page. Except to the bibliographer, it is probably no loss that the fourth edition has not been accessible, for the careful collation made of the four accessible editions shows not a variant among them which affects the sense of the text. In spite of many typographical faults, the first octavo evidently gave the sense of Goldsmith's play accurately. The later octavos merely correct faulty type and incorrect spellings.

This edition gives, for the first time, a reprint of the eighteenth century spelling and recovers Goldsmith's texts from oversights and unnecessary emendations of his editors. In capitalization, punctuation, etc., the text has been treated like that of *The Good Natur'd Man*.

G. P. B.

TO SAMUEL JOHNSON, L.L.D.[1]

DEAR SIR,

By inscribing this slight performance to you, I do not mean so much to compliment you as myself. It may do me some honour to inform the public, that I have lived many years in intimacy with you. It may serve the interests of mankind also to inform them, that the greatest wit may be found in a character, without impairing the most unaffected piety.

I have, particularly, reason to thank you for your partiality to this performance. The undertaking a comedy, not merely sentimental, was very dangerous;[2] and Mr. Colman, who saw this piece in its various stages, always thought it so. However, I ventured to trust it to the public; and, though it was necessarily delayed till late in the season,[3] I have every reason to be grateful.

I am, dear sir,
Your most sincere friend
And admirer,

OLIVER GOLDSMITH

[1] For Johnson's connection with *She Stoops to Conquer* see "Introduction," p. 20.

[2] Very dangerous, by reason of the temporary popularity of sentimental comedy.

[3] Late in the season, when there could be but few representations. The season ended May 31st, before which date the play was acted twelve times.

PROLOGUE

By David Garrick, Esq.

Enter Mr. Woodward,[4] *dressed in black,*
and holding a handkerchief to his eyes.

Excuse me, sirs, I pray—I can't yet speak—
I'm crying now—and have been all the week!
'Tis not alone this mourning suit, good masters;
I've that within[5]—for which there are no plaisters!
Pray wou'd you know the reason why I'm crying?
The Comic Muse, long sick, is now a dying!
And if she goes, my tears will never stop;
For as a play'r, I can't squeeze out one drop:
I am undone, that's all—shall lose my bread—
I'd rather, but that's nothing—lose my head.
When the sweet maid is laid upon the bier,
Shuter and *I* shall be chief mourners here.
To *her* a mawkish drab of spurious breed,
Who deals in *sentimentals,* will succeed!
Poor *Ned*[6] and *I* are dead to all intents,
We can as soon speak *Greek as sentiments!*
Both nervous grown, to keep our spirits up,
We now and then take down a hearty cup.
What shall we do?—If Comedy forsake us!
They'll turn us out, and no one else will take us;
But why can't I be moral?—Let me try—
My heart thus pressing—fix'd my face and eye—
With a sententious look, that nothing means,
(Faces are blocks in sentimental scenes),
Thus I begin—*All is not gold that glitters,*[7]
Pleasure seems sweet, but proves a glass of bitters.
When ign'rance enters, folly is at hand;
Learning is better far than house and land.

[4] Henry Woodward (1717-77) had no part in this piece.
(See *Dramatis Personæ* of the *Good Natur'd Man.*)

[5] *Hamlet,* Act I. Sc. 2.

[6] Edward Shuter (1728-76), who acted Mr. Hardcastle. Both
Shuter and Woodward were eminent comic actors. Garrick
thought Shuter "the greatest comic genius he had ever seen."

[7] Dryden's *Hind and Panther.* Bartlett's *Familiar Quotations*
gives other sources.

Let not your virtue trip, who trips may stumble,
And virtue is not virtue, if she tumble.
   I give it up—morals won't do for me;
To make you laugh I must play tragedy.
One hope remains—hearing the maid was ill,
A *doctor* comes this night to shew his skill.
To cheer her heart, and give your muscles motion,
He in *five draughts* prepar'd, presents a potion·
A kind of magic charm—for be assur'd,
If you will *swallow* it, the maid is cur'd.
But desp'rate the Doctor, and her case is,
If you reject the dose, and make wry faces!
This truth he boasts, will boast it while he lives,
No *pois'nous drugs* are mix'd in what he gives;
Should he succeed, you'll give him his degree;
If not, within he will receive no fee!
The college *you*,[8] must his pretensions back,
Pronounce him *regular*, or dub him *quack*.

[8] This means that, in this case, the audience stood in place of the College of Physicians.

DRAMATIS PERSONÆ

MEN

Sir Charles Marlow
Young Marlow (*his Son*)
Hardcastle
Hastings
Tony Lumpkin
Diggory

WOMEN

Mrs. Hardcastle
Miss Hardcastle
Miss Neville
Maid

Landlords, Servants, &c., &c.

SHE STOOPS TO CONQUER;

OR,

The Mistakes of a Night[9]

ACT I

SCENE I—*A Chamber in an old-fashioned House*

Enter Mrs. Hardcastle *and* Mr. Hardcastle.

MRS. HARDCASTLE. I vow, Mr. Hardcastle, you're very particular. Is there a creature in the whole country but ourselves that does not take a trip to town now and then, to rub off the rust a little? There's the two Miss Hoggs, and our neighbour, Mrs. Grigsby, go to take a month's polishing every winter.

Hardcastle. Ay, and bring back vanity and affectation to last them the whole year. I wonder why London cannot keep its own fools at home. In my time, the follies of the town crept slowly among us, but now they travel faster than a stage-coach. Its fopperies come down, not only as inside passengers, but in the very basket.

Mrs. Hardcastle. Ay, *your* times were fine times, indeed; you have been telling us of *them* for many a long year. Here we live in an old rumbling[10] mansion, that looks for all the world like an inn, but that we never see company. Our best visitors are old Mrs. Oddfish, the curate's wife, and little Cripplegate, the lame dancing-master: and all our entertainment your old stories of Prince Eugene[11] and the Duke of Marlborough. I hate such old-fashioned trumpery.

Hardcastle. And I love it. I love every thing that's old:

[9] For the tentative titles of the play, see "Introduction," p. 21.

[10] Probably a misprint for rambling.

[11] Prince Eugene of Savoy (1663-1736) was the ally of Marlborough at Blenheim (1704), Oudenarde (1708), and Malplaquet (1709).

old friends, old times, old manners, old books, old wine;[12] and, I believe, Dorothy [*taking her hand*], you'll own I have been pretty fond of an old wife.

Mrs. Hardcastle. Lord, Mr. Hardcastle, you're for ever at your Dorothy's and your old wife's. You may be a Darby, but I'll be no Joan,[13] I promise you. I'm not so old as you'd make me by more than one good year. Add twenty to twenty, and make money of that.

Hardcastle. Let me see; twenty added to twenty—makes just fifty and seven!

Mrs. Hardcastle. It's false, Mr. Hardcastle: I was but twenty when I was brought to bed of Tony, that I had by Mr. Lumpkin, my first husband; and he's not come to years of discretion yet.

Hardcastle. Nor ever will, I dare answer for him. Ay, you have taught *him* finely!

Mrs. Hardcastle. No matter, Tony Lumpkin has a good fortune. My son is not to live by his learning. I don't think a boy wants much learning to spend fifteen hundred a year.

Hardcastle. Learning, quotha! A mere composition of tricks and mischief!

Mrs. Hardcastle. Humour, my dear: nothing but humour. Come, Mr. Hardcastle, you must allow the boy a little humour.

Hardcastle. I'd sooner allow him a horse-pond! If burning the footmens shoes, frighting[14] the maids, and worrying the kittens, be humour, he has it. It was but yesterday he fastened my wig to the back of my chair, and when I went to make a bow, I popt my bald head in Mrs. Frizzle's face![15]

Mrs. Hardcastle. And am I to blame? The poor boy was always too sickly to do any good. A school would be his death. When he comes to be a little stronger, who knows what a year or two's Latin may do for him?

[12] Old friends . . . old wine. In Bacon's *Apothegms*, No. 97, this sentiment is attributed to Alonso of Arragon. Several variations of it appear in Bartlett's *Familiar Quotations*.

[13] Darby and Joan are the types of a contented couple. There is an old song on them in the *Gentleman's Magazine* for March, 1735 (V. 153).

[14] *frighting*, octavos; recent editions, frightening.

[15] Lord Clare's daughter played this trick on Goldsmith himself (Forster's *Life*, bk. IV. ch. 15).

Hardcastle. Latin for him! A cat and fiddle! No, no, the ale-house and the stable are the only schools he'll ever go to.

Mrs. Hardcastle. Well, we must not snub the poor boy now, for I believe we shan't have him long among us. Any body that looks in his face may see he's consumptive.

Hardcastle. Ay, if growing too fat be one of the symptoms.

Mrs. Hardcastle. He coughs sometimes.

Hardcastle. Yes, when his liquor goes the wrong way.

Mrs. Hardcastle. I'm actually afraid of his lungs.

Hardcastle. And truly, so am I; for he sometimes whoops like a speaking trumpet—[TONY *hallooing behind the scenes.*]—O, there he goes—A very consumptive figure, truly!

Enter TONY, *crossing the stage.*

Mrs. Hardcastle. Tony, where are you going, my charmer? Won't you give papa and I a little of your company, lovee?

Tony. I'm in haste, mother, I cannot stay.

Mrs. Hardcastle. You shan't venture out this raw evening, my dear: you look most shockingly.

Tony. I can't stay, I tell you. *The Three Pigeons* expects me down every moment. There's some fun going forward.

Hardcastle. Ay; the ale-house, the old place: I thought so.

Mrs. Hardcastle. A low, paltry set of fellows.

Tony. Not so low, neither. There's Dick Muggins, the exciseman; Jack Slang, the horse doctor; Little Aminadab, that grinds the music box; and Tom Twist, that spins the pewter platter.[16]

Mrs. Hardcastle. Pray, my dear, disappoint them for one night, at least.

Tony. As for disappointing *them,* I should not so much mind;[17] but I can't abide to disappoint *myself.*

Mrs. Hardcastle [*Detaining him*]. You shan't go.

Tony. I will, I tell you.

Mrs. Hardcastle. I say you shan't.

---

[16] "One begged to be heard while he gave *Death and the Lady* in high taste; another sung to a plate which he kept trundling on the edges" (*Essays*, 1765, 25).

[17] *much mind,* octavos; recent editions omit so.

Tony. We'll see which is strongest, you or I.

[*Exit, hawling her out.*

HARDCASTLE, *solus.*

Hardcastle. Ay, there goes a pair that only spoil each other. But is not the whole age in a combination to drive sense and discretion out of doors? There's my pretty darling, Kate; the fashions of the times have almost infected her too. By living a year or two in town, she is as fond of gauze and French frippery as the best of them.

Enter MISS HARDCASTLE.

Hardcastle. Blessings on my pretty innocence! Drest out as usual, my Kate! Goodness! What a quantity of superfluous silk hast thou got about thee, girl! I could never teach the fools of this age that the indigent world [18] could be cloathed out of the trimmings of the vain.

Miss Hardcastle. You know our agreement, sir. You allow me the morning to receive and pay visits, and to dress in my own manner; and in the evening, I put on my housewife's dress, to please you.

Hardcastle. Well, remember, I insist on the terms of our agreement; and, by-the-bye, I believe I shall have occasion to try your obedience this very evening.

Miss Hardcastle. I protest, sir, I don't comprehend your meaning.

Hardcastle. Then, to be plain with you, Kate, I expect the young gentleman I have chosen to be your husband from town this very day. I have his father's letter, in which he informs me his son is set out, and that he intends to follow himself shortly after.

Miss Hardcastle. Indeed! I wish I had known something of this before. Bless me, how shall I behave? It's a thousand to one I shan't like him; our meeting will be so formal, and so like a thing of business that I shall find no room for friendship or esteem.

Hardcastle. Depend upon it, child, I'll never controul your choice; but Mr. Marlow, whom I have pitched upon, is the son of my old friend, Sir Charles Marlow, of whom you have heard me talk so often. The young gentleman has been bred a scholar, and is designed for an employment in the service of his country. I am told he's a man of an excellent understanding.

---

[18] There is a similar thought in the *Vicar of Wakefield*, ch. IV.

Miss Hardcastle. Is he?

Hardcastle. Very generous.

Miss Hardcastle. I believe I shall like him.

Hardcastle. Young and brave.

Miss Hardcastle. I'm sure I shall like him.

Hardcastle. And very handsome.

Miss Hardcastle. My dear papa, say no more [*Kissing his hand*], he's mine, I'll have him!

Hardcastle. And, to crown all, Kate, he's one of the most bashful and reserved young fellows in all the world.

Miss Hardcastle. Eh! you have frozen me to death again. That word *reserved* has undone all the rest of his accomplishments. A reserved lover, it is said, always makes a suspicious husband.

Hardcastle. On the contrary, modesty seldom resides in a breast that is not enriched with nobler virtues. It was the very feature in his character that first struck me.

Miss Hardcastle. He must have more striking features to catch me, I promise you. However, if he be so young, so handsome, and so everything, as you mention, I believe he'll do still. I think I'll have him.

Hardcastle. Ay, Kate, but there is still an obstacle. Its more than an even wager, he may not have *you*.

Miss Hardcastle. My dear papa, why will you mortify one so?—Well, if he refuses, instead of breaking my heart at his indifference, I'll only break my glass for its flattery. Set my cap to some newer fashion, and look out for some less difficult admirer.

Hardcastle. Bravely resolved! In the mean time, I'll go prepare the servants for his reception; as we seldom see company, they want as much training as a company of recruits the first day's muster.   [*Exit.*

Miss Hardcastle, *sola.*

Miss Hardcastle. Lud, this news of papa's puts me all in a flutter. *Young, handsome;* these he put last; but I put them foremost. *Sensible, good-natured;* I like all that. But then *reserved*, and *sheepish*, that's much against him. Yet, can't he be cured of his timidity by being taught to be proud of his wife? Yes, and can't I—But I vow I'm disposing of the husband before I have secured the lover!

Enter Miss Neville.

Miss Hardcastle. I'm glad you're come, Neville, my

dear. Tell me, Constance, how do I look this evening? Is there any thing whimsical about me? Is it one of my well looking days, child? Am I in face today? [19]

Miss Neville. Perfectly, my dear. Yet, now I look again —bless me!—surely no accident has happened among the canary birds or the gold-fishes? Has your brother or the cat been meddling? Or has the last novel been too moving?

Miss Hardcastle. No; nothing of all this. I have been threatened—I can scarce get it out—I have been threatened with a lover!

Miss Neville. And his name—

Miss Hardcastle. Is Marlow.

Miss Neville. Indeed!

Miss Hardcastle. The son of Sir Charles Marlow.

Miss Neville. As I live, the most intimate friend of Mr. Hastings, *my* admirer. They are never asunder. I believe you must have seen him when we lived in town.

Miss Hardcastle. Never.

Miss Neville. He's a very singular character, I assure you. Among women of reputation and virtue, he is the modestest man alive; but his acquaintance give him a very different character among creatures of another stamp: you understand me.

Miss Hardcastle. An odd character, indeed! I shall never be able to manage him. What shall I do? Pshaw, think no more of him, but trust to occurrences for success. But how goes on your own affair, my dear? Has my mother been courting you for my brother Tony, as usual?

Miss Neville. I have just come from one of our agreeable *tête-à-têtes.* She has been saying a hundred tender things, and setting off her pretty monster as the very pink of perfection.

Miss Hardcastle. And her partiality is such that she actually thinks him so. A fortune like your's is no small temptation. Besides, as she has the sole management of it, I'm not surprized to see her unwilling to let it go out of the family.

Miss Neville. A fortune like mine, which chiefly consists in jewels, is no such mighty temptation. But at any rate, if my dear Hastings be but constant, I make no doubt to be too hard for her at last. However, I let her suppose that

[19] Am I looking my best today? *New English Dictionary* compares, Am I in voice?

I am in love with her son, and she never once dreams that my affections are fixed upon another.

Miss Hardcastle. My good brother holds out stoutly. I could almost love him for hating you so.

Miss Neville. It is a good natured creature at bottom, and I'm sure would wish to see me married to any body but himself. But my aunt's bell rings for our afternoon's walk round the improvements.[20] *Allons.* Courage is necessary, as our affairs are critical.

Miss Hardcastle. Would it were bed time[21] and all were well.   [*Exeunt.*

SCENE 2—*An alehouse room. Several shabby fellows, with punch and tobacco. TONY at the head of the table, a little higher than the rest: a mallet in his hand.*

OMNES. Hurrea, hurrea, hurrea, bravo!

First Fellow. Now, gentlemen, silence for a song. The 'Squire is going to knock himself down for a song.[22]

Omnes. Ay, a song, a song.

Tony. Then I'll sing you, gentlemen, a song I made upon this ale-house, *The Three Pigeons.*[23]

SONG

> Let school-masters puzzle their brain,
>   With grammar, and nonsense, and learning;
> Good liquor, I stoutly maintain,
>   Gives genus a better discerning,
> Let them brag of their Heathenish Gods,
>   Their Lethes, their Styxes, and Stygians;
> Their Quis, and their Quæs, and their Quods,
>   They're all but a parcel of Pigeons.
>
>   Toroddle, toroddle, toroll!
>
> When Methodist preachers[24] come down,
>   A preaching that drinking is sinful,
> I'll wager the rascals a crown,

[20] *Round the improvements*, octavos; but modern editions, through.

[21] I *Henry IV.*, Act v. Sc. 1.

[22] Call upon himself for a song.

[23] Goldsmith himself was in the habit of singing this capital song (Birkbeck Hill's *Boswell's Johnson*, 1887, II, 219).

[24] Goldsmith, here and elsewhere, shows imperfect sympathy with the followers of Wesley and Whitefield.

> *They always preach best with a skinful.*
> *But when you come down with your pence,*
> *For a slice of their scurvy religion,*
> *I'll leave it to all men of sense,*
>> *But you, my good friend, are the pigeon.*
>>>> Toroddle, toroddle, toroll!

> *Then come, put the jorum about,*
>> *And let us be merry and clever,*
> *Our hearts and our liquors are stout,*
>> *Here's the Three Jolly Pigeons for ever.*
> *Let some cry up woodcock or hare,*
>> *Your bustards, your ducks, and your widgeons;*
> *But of all the birds[25] in the air,*
>> *Here's a health to the Three Jolly Pigeons.*
>>>> Toroddle, toroddle, toroll!

Omnes. Bravo, bravo!

First Fellow. The 'Squire has got spunk in him.

Second Fellow. I loves to hear him sing, bekeays he never gives us nothing that's *low*.[26]

Third Fellow. O damn any thing that's *low*, I cannot bear it!

Fourth Fellow. The genteel thing is the genteel thing at any time. If so be that a gentleman bees in a concatenation accordingly.

Third Fellow. I like the maxum of it, Master Muggins. What, tho' I am obligated to dance a bear, a man may be a gentleman for all that. May this be my poison if my bear ever dances but to the very genteelest of tunes. *Water Parted*,[27] or the minuet in *Ariadne*.[28]

Second Fellow. What a pity it is the 'Squire is not come to his own. It would be well for all the publicans within ten miles round of him.

Tony. Ecod, and so it would, Master Slang. I'd then shew what it was to keep choice of company.

[25] Some later editions read *gay birds,* but there is no sanction for this in the octavos.

[26] See "Introduction," p. 14.

[27] A song sung by Arbaces in Arne's opera of *Artaxerxes,* 1762, beginning,—

> "Water parted from the sea
>> May increase the river's tide," etc.

[28] *Ariadne* was an opera by Handel, at the end of the **over-**ture to which came a famous minuet.

Second Fellow. O, he takes after his own father for that. To be sure, old 'Squire Lumpkin was the finest gentleman I ever set my eyes on. For winding the streight horn, or beating a thicket for a hare, or a wench, he never had his fellow. It was a saying in the place that he kept the best horses, dogs, and girls in the whole county.

Tony. Ecod, and when I'm of age, I'll be no bastard, I promise you. I have been thinking of Bett Bouncer and the miller's grey mare to begin with. But come, my boys, drink about and be merry, for you pay no reckoning. Well, Stingo, what's the matter?

Enter LANDLORD.

Landlord. There be two gentlemen in a post-chaise at the door. They have lost their way upo' the forest; and they are talking something about Mr. Hardcastle.

Tony. As sure as can be, one of them must be the gentleman that's coming down to court my sister. Do they seem to be Londoners?

Landlord. I believe they may. They look woundily like Frenchmen.

Tony. Then desire them to step this way, and I'll set them right in a twinkling. [*Exit* LANDLORD.] Gentlemen, as they mayn't be good enough company for you, step down for a moment, and I'll be with you in the squeezing of a lemon.   [*Exeunt Mob.*

TONY *solus.*

Tony. Father-in-law has been calling me whelp and hound, this half year. Now, if I pleased, I could be so revenged upon the old grumbletonian. But then I'm afraid —afraid of what? I shall soon be worth fifteen hundred a year, and let him frighten me out of *that* if he can!

Enter LANDLORD, *conducting* MARLOW *and* HASTINGS.

Marlow. What a tedious, uncomfortable day have we had of it! We were told it was but forty miles across the country, and we have come above threescore!

Hastings. And all, Marlow, from that unaccountable reserve of yours, that would not let us enquire more frequently on the way.

Marlow. I own, Hastings, I am unwilling to lay myself under an obligation to every one I meet; and often stand the chance of an unmannerly answer.

Hastings. At present, however, we are not likely to receive any answer.

Tony. No offence, gentlemen. But I'm told you have been enquiring for one Mr. Hardcastle, in these parts.[29] Do you know what part of the country you are in?

Hastings. Not in the least, sir, but should thank you for information.

Tony. Nor the way you came?

Hastings. No, sir; but if you can inform us—

Tony. Why, gentlemen, if you know neither the road you are going, nor where you are, nor the road you came, the first thing I have to inform you is, that—you have lost your way.

Marlow. We wanted no ghost to tell us that.[30]

Tony. Pray, gentlemen, may I be so bold as to ask the place from whence you came?

Marlow. That's not necessary towards directing us where we are to go.

Tony. No offence; but question for question is all fair, you know. Pray, gentlemen, is not this same Hardcastle a cross-grain'd, old-fashion'd, whimsical fellow with an ugly face, a daughter, and a pretty son?

Hastings. We have not seen the gentleman, but he has the family you mention.

Tony. The daughter, a tall, trapesing, trolloping, talkative maypole— The son, a pretty, well-bred, agreeable youth, that every body is fond of!

Marlow. Our information differs in this. The daughter is said to be well-bred and beautiful; the son, an aukward booby, reared up and spoiled at his mother's apron-string.

Tony. He-he-hem—then, gentlemen, all I have to tell you is, that you won't reach Mr. Hardcastle's house this night, I believe.

Hastings. Unfortunate!

Tony. It's a damn'd long, dark, boggy, dirty, dangerous way. Stingo, tell the gentlemen the way to Mr. Hardcastle's;—[*winking upon the* LANDLORD,] Mr. Hardcastle's of Quagmire Marsh, you understand me.

Landlord. Master Hardcastle's! Lack-a-daisy,[31] my mas-

---

[29] *These parts;* octavos, those.
[30] *Hamlet,* Act I. Sc. 5.
[31] *Lack-a-daisy;* octavos, lock-a-daisy.

ters, you're come a deadly deal wrong! When you came to the bottom of the hill, you should have cross'd down Squash-lane.

Marlow. Cross down Squash-lane!

Landlord. Then you were to keep streight forward 'till you came to four roads.

Marlow. Come to where four roads meet!

Tony. Ay, but you must be sure to take only one of them.

Marlow. O, sir, you're facetious.

Tony. Then, keeping to the right, you are to go sideways till you come upon Crack-skull Common: there you must look sharp for the track of the wheel, and go forward 'till you come to Farmer Murrain's barn. Coming to the farmer's barn, you are to turn to the right, and then to the left, and then to the right about again, till you find out the old mill—

Marlow. Zounds, man, we could as soon find out the longitude! [32]

Hastings. What's to be done, Marlow?

Marlow. This house promises but a poor reception; though, perhaps, the landlord can accommodate us.

Landlord. Alack, master, we have but one spare bed in the whole house.

Tony. And to my knowledge, that's taken up by three lodgers already. [*After a pause in which the rest seem disconcerted.*] I have hit it. Don't you think, Stingo, our landlady could accommodate the gentlemen, by the fireside, with—three chairs and a bolster?

Hastings. I hate sleeping by the fire-side.

Marlow. And I detest your three chairs and a bolster.

Tony. You do, do you?—then let me see—what—if you go on a mile further, to the Buck's Head; the old Buck's Head on the hill, one of the best inns in the whole county?

Hastings. O ho! [33] so we have escaped an adventure for this night, however.

---

[32] "Find out the longitude" was a popular enquiry in the eighteenth century, eventually solved by John Harrison of Foulby in Yorkshire, who received the reward of £20,000 which, under an act of Queen Anne, Government was empowered to pay to the discoverer.

[33] *O ho!* octavos. Recent editions read: Oh, oh!

Landlord [*Apart to* TONY]. Sure, you ben't sending them to your father's as an inn,[34] be you?

Tony. Mum, you fool, you. Let *them* find that out. [*To them.*] You have only to keep on streight forward till you come to a large old house by the roadside. You'll see a pair of large horns over the door. That's the sign. Drive up the yard, and call stoutly about you.

Hastings. Sir, we are obliged to you. The servants can't miss the way?

Tony. No, no; but I tell you, though, the landlord is rich, and going to leave off business; so he wants to be thought a gentleman, saving your presence, he! he! he! He'll be for giving you his company, and, ecod, if you mind him, he'll persuade you that his mother was an alderman, and his aunt a justice of peace! [35]

Landlord. A troublesome old blade, to be sure; but a keeps as good wines and beds as any in the whole country.

Marlow. Well, if he supplies us with these, we shall want no further connexion. We are to turn to the right, did you say?

Tony. No, no; streight forward. I'll just step myself and shew you a piece of the way. [*To the* LANDLORD.] Mum.

Landlord. Ah, bless your heart, for a sweet, pleasant— damn'd mischievous son of a whore.   [*Exeunt.*

ACT II

SCENE—*An old-fashioned House*

Enter HARDCASTLE, *followed by three or four aukward* Servants.

HARDCASTLE. Well, I hope you're perfect in the table exercise I have been teaching you these three days. You all know your posts and your places, and can shew that you have been used to good company without ever stirring from home.

Omnes. Ay, ay.

[34] This was a recollection of an actual incident in Goldsmith's youth. While travelling to school at Edgeworthstown, he had been hoaxed into mistaking the house of a gentleman at Ardagh for an inn (Forster's *Life*, bk. i.)

[35] *Justice of peace*, octavos; some recent editions, of the peace.

Hardcastle. When company comes, you are not to pop out and stare, and then run in again, like frighted [36] rabbits in a warren.

Omnes. No, no.

Hardcastle. You, Diggory, whom I have taken from the barn, are to make a shew at the side-table; and you, Roger, whom I have advanced from the plough, are to place yourself behind *my* chair. But you're not to stand so, with your hands in your pockets. Take your hands from your pockets, Roger; and from your head, you blockhead, you. See how Diggory carries his hands. They're a little too stiff, indeed, but that's no great matter.

Diggory. Ay, mind how I hold them. I learned to hold my hands this way, when I was upon drill for the militia. And so being upon drill—

Hardcastle. You must not be so talkative, Diggory. You must be all attention to the guests. You must hear us talk, and not think of talking; you must see us drink, and not think of drinking; you must see us eat, and not think of eating.

Diggory. By the laws, your worship, that's parfectly unpossible. Whenever Diggory sees yeating going forward, ecod, he's always wishing for a mouthful himself.

Hardcastle. Blockhead! Is not a belly-full in the kitchen as good as a belly-full in the parlour? Stay your stomach with that reflection.

Diggory. Ecod, I thank your worship, I'll make a shift to stay my stomach with a slice of cold beef in the pantry.

Hardcastle. Diggory, you are too talkative. Then, if I happen to say a good thing, or tell a good story at table, you must not all burst out a-laughing, as if you made part of the company.

Diggory. Then, ecod, your worship must not tell the story of Ould Grouse in the gun-room:[37] I can't help laughing at that—he! he! he!—for the soul of me! We have laughed at that these twenty years—ha! ha! ha!

Hardcastle. Ha! ha! ha! The story is a good one. Well, honest Diggory, you may laugh at that—but still remember to be attentive. Suppose one of the company should call for a glass of wine, how will you behave? A glass of wine, sir, if you please [*to* DIGGORY]—Eh, why don't you move?

[36] *Frighted*, octavos; recent editions, frightened.
[37] This story has never been traced.

Diggory. Ecod, your worship, I never have courage till I see the eatables and drinkables brought upo' the table, and then I'm as bauld as a lion.

Hardcastle. What, will no body move?

First Servant. I'm not to leave this pleace.

Second Servant. I'm sure it's no pleace of mine.

Third Servant. Nor mine, for sartain.

Diggory. Wauns, and I'm sure it canna be mine.

Hardcastle. You numbskulls! and so, while, like your betters, you are quarrelling for places, the guests must be starved. O you dunces! I find I must begin all over again—but don't I hear a coach drive into the yard? To your posts, you blockheads! I'll go in the mean time and give my old friend's son a hearty reception at the gate.

[*Exit* HARDCASTLE.

Diggory. By the elevens, my pleace is gone quite out of my head!

Roger. I know that my pleace is to be every where!

First Servant. Where the devil is mine?

Second Servant. My pleace is to be no where at all; and so Ize go about my business!

[*Exeunt* SERVANTS, *running about as if frighted, different ways.*

Enter SERVANT[38] *with candles, shewing in*
MARLOW *and* HASTINGS.

Servant. Welcome, gentlemen, very welcome. This way.

Hastings. After the disappointments of the day, welcome once more, Charles, to the comforts of a clean room and a good fire. Upon my word, a very well-looking house; antique but creditable.

Marlow. The usual fate of a large mansion. Having first ruined the master by good housekeeping, it at last comes to levy contributions as an inn.

Hastings. As you say, we passengers are to be taxed to pay all these fineries. I have often seen a good side-board, or a marble chimney-piece, tho' not actually put in the bill, enflame a reckoning confoundedly.

Marlow. Travelers, George, must pay in all places. The only difference is that in good inns you pay dearly for luxuries; in bad inns you are fleeced and starved.

[38] Roger apparently.

Hastings. You have lived pretty much among them. In truth, I have been often surprized that you who have seen so much of the world, with your natural good sense, and your many opportunities, could never yet acquire a requisite share of assurance.

Marlow. The Englishman's malady. But tell me, George, where could I have learned that assurance you talk of? My life has been chiefly spent in a college, or an inn, in seclusion from that lovely part of the creation that chiefly teach men confidence. I don't know that I was ever familiarly acquainted with a single modest woman—except my mother—But among females of another class, you know—

Hastings. Ay, among them you are impudent enough of all conscience!

Marlow. They are of *us*, you know.

Hastings. But in the company of women of reputation I never saw such an ideot, such a trembler; you look for all the world as if you wanted an opportunity of stealing out of the room.

Marlow. Why, man, that's because I *do* want to steal out of the room. Faith, I have often formed a resolution to break the ice, and rattle away at any rate. But I don't know how, a single glance from a pair of fine eyes has totally overset my resolutions. An impudent fellow may counterfeit modesty, but I'll be hanged if a modest man can ever counterfeit impudence.

Hastings. If you could but say half the fine things to them that I have heard you lavish upon the barmaid of an inn, or even a college bed maker—

Marlow. Why, George, I can't say fine things to them. They freeze, they petrify me. They may talk of a comet, or a burning mountain, or some such bagatelle. But to me, a modest woman, drest out in all her finery, is the most tremendous object of the whole creation.

Hastings. Ha! ha! ha! At this rate, man, how can you ever expect to marry!

Marlow. Never, unless, as among kings and princes, my bride were to be courted by proxy. If, indeed, like an Eastern bridegroom, one were to be introduced to a wife he never saw before, it might be endured. But to go through all the terrors of a formal courtship, together with the episode of aunts, grandmothers and cousins, and at last to blurt out the broad, staring question of, *Madam, will you marry me?* No, no, that's a strain much above me, I assure you!

Hastings. I pity you. But how do you intend behaving to the lady you are come down to visit at the request of your father?

Marlow. As I behave to all other ladies. Bow very low. Answer yes, or no, to all her demands—But for the rest, I don't think I shall venture to look in her face till I see my father's again.

Hastings. I'm surprized that one who is so warm a friend can be so cool a lover.

Marlow. To be explicit, my dear Hastings, my chief inducement down was to be instrumental in forwarding your happiness, not my own. Miss Neville loves you, the family don't know you, as my friend you are sure of a reception, and let honour do the rest.

Hastings. My dear Marlow! But I'll suppress the emotion. Were I a wretch, meanly seeking to carry off a fortune, you should be the last man in the world I would apply to for assistance. But Miss Neville's person is all I ask, and that is mine, both from her deceased father's consent and her own inclination.

Marlow. Happy man! You have talents and art to captivate any woman. I'm doom'd to adore the sex, and yet to converse with the only part of it I despise. This stammer in my address, and this aukward, prepossessing[39] visage of mine, can never permit me to soar above the reach of a milliner's 'prentice, or one of the dutchesses of Drury-lane.[40] Pshaw, this fellow here to interrupt us!

Enter HARDCASTLE.

Hardcastle. Gentlemen, once more you are heartily welcome. Which is Mr. Marlow? Sir, you're heartily welcome. It's not my way, you see, to receive my friends with my back to the fire. I like to give them a hearty re-

[39] As the reverse is meant, modern editions print unprepossessing.

[40] Women of the town, who often passed themselves off at public places as persons of quality. In the Description of an Author's Bedchamber (*Citizen of the World*, 1762, XXIX.) Goldsmith speaks of the "drabs . . . of Drury Lane." See also essay on Scotch Marriages, p. 105 of this volume.

ception, in the old stile, at my gate. I like to see their horses and trunks taken care of.

Marlow [*Aside*]. He has got our names from the servants already. [*To him.*] We approve your caution and hospitality, sir. [*To* HASTINGS.] I have been thinking, George, of changing our travelling dresses in the morning. I am grown confoundedly ashamed of mine.

Hardcastle. I beg, Mr. Marlow, you'll use no ceremony in this house.

Hastings. I fancy, George, you're right: the first blow is half the battle. I intend opening the campaign with the white and gold.

Hardcastle. Mr. Marlow—Mr. Hastings—gentlemen— pray be under no constraint in this house. This is Liberty-hall, gentlemen. You may do just as you please here.

Marlow. Yet, George, if we open the campaign too fiercely at first, we may want ammunition before it is over. I think to reserve the embroidery to secure a retreat.

Hardcastle. Your talking of a retreat, Mr. Marlow, puts me in mind of the Duke of Marlborough, when we went to besiege Denain.[41] He first summoned the garrison—

Marlow. Don't you think the *ventre dor* waistcoat will do with the plain brown?

Hardcastle. He first summoned the garrison, which might consist of about five thousand men—

Hastings. I think not: brown and yellow mix but very poorly.

Hardcastle. I say, gentlemen, as I was telling you, he summoned the garrison, which might consist of about five thousand men—

Marlow. The girls like finery.

Hardcastle. Which might consist of about five thousand men, well appointed with stores,[42] ammunition, and other implements of war. "Now," says the Duke of Marlborough to George Brooks, that stood next to him—you must have heard of George Brooks; "I'll pawn my dukedom," says he, "but I take that garrison without spilling a drop of blood!" So—

Marlow. What, my good friend, if you gave us a glass

[41] This French town (Dep. du Nord) is chiefly famous in history for the victory of Marshal Villars over the Allies under Eugene (1712).

[42] O1 misprints, stones.

of punch in the mean time; it would help us to carry on the siege with vigour.

Hardcastle [*Aside*]. Punch, sir!—This is the most unaccountable kind of modesty I ever met with!

Marlow. Yes, sir, punch! A glass of warm punch, after our journey, will be comfortable. This is Liberty-hall, you know.

Hardcastle. Here's cup,[43] sir.

Marlow [*Aside*]. So this fellow, in his Liberty-hall, will only let us have just what he pleases.

Hardcastle [*Taking the cup*]. I hope you'll find it to your mind. I have prepared it with my own hands, and I believe you'll own the ingredients are tolerable. Will you be so good as to pledge me, sir? Here, Mr. Marlow, here is to our better acquaintance!   [*Drinks.*

Marlow [*Aside*]. A very impudent fellow this! But he's a character, and I'll humour him a little.—Sir, my service to you.   [*Drinks.*

Hastings [*Aside*]. I see this fellow wants to give us his company, and forgets that he's an innkeeper before he has learned to be a gentleman.

Marlow. From the excellence of your cup, my old friend, I suppose you have a good deal of business in this part of the country. Warm work, now and then, at elections, I suppose?

Hardcastle. No, sir, I have long given that work over. Since our betters have hit upon the expedient of electing each other, there's no business *for us that sell ale*.[44]

Hastings. So, then you have no turn for politics, I find.

Hardcastle. Not in the least. There was a time, indeed, I fretted myself about the mistakes of government, like other people; but, finding myself every day grow more angry, and the government growing no better, I left it to mend itself. Since that, I no more trouble my head about *Heyder Ally*,[45] or *Ally Cawn*,[46] than about *Ally Croaker*.[47] Sir, my service to you.

---

[43] *Here's cup*, octavos; some later editions read wrongly, *Here's a cup*.

[44] This has been explained as meaning "us that give ale for votes." But it also helps the confusion of Hardcastle with a landlord.

[45] Sultan of Mysore, 1717-82.

[46] Subah of Bengal.

[47] A popular Irish song, dating from 1753, a verse of which is quoted in ch. v. of Miss Edgeworth's *Belinda*.

Hastings. So that, with eating above stairs, and drinking below, with receiving your friends within, and amusing them without, you lead a good, pleasant, bustling life of it.

Hardcastle. I do stir about a great deal, that's certain. Half the differences of the parish are adjusted in this very parlour.

Marlow [After drinking]. And you have an argument in your cup, old gentleman, better than any in Westminster-hall.[48]

Hardcastle. Ay, young gentleman, that, and a little philosophy.

Marlow [Aside]. Well, this is the first time I ever heard of an innkeeper's philosophy.

Hastings. So then, like an experienced general, you attack them on every quarter. If you find their reason manageable, you attack it with your philosophy; if you find they have no reason, you attack them with this. Here's your health, my philosopher.   [*Drinks.*

Hardcastle. Good, very good, thank you; ha! ha! Your generalship puts me in mind of Prince Eugene, when he fought the Turks at the battle of Belgrade.[49] You shall hear—

Marlow. Instead of the battle of Belgrade, I believe it's almost time to talk about supper. What has your philosophy got in the house for supper?

Hardcastle [Aside]. For supper, sir!—Was ever such a request to a man in his own house!

Marlow. Yes, sir, supper, sir; I begin to feel an appetite. I shall make devilish work to-night in the larder, I promise you.

Hardcastle [Aside]. Such a brazen dog, sure, never my eyes beheld. [*To him.*] Why, really, sir, as for supper I can't well tell. My Dorothy, and the cook maid, settle these things between them. I leave these kind of things entirely to them.

Marlow. You do, do you?

Hardcastle. Entirely. By-the-bye, I believe they are in actual consultation upon what's for supper this moment in the kitchen.

Marlow. Then I beg they'll admit *me* as one of their

[48] Till 1882 the Law Courts met here.
[49] 1717. Goldsmith must often have heard the story of this from General Oglethorpe, who had been present.

privy council. It's a way I have got. When I travel, I always chuse to regulate my own supper. Let the cook be called. No offence, I hope, sir.

Hardcastle. O, no, sir, none in the least; yet, I don't know how: our Bridget, the cook maid, is not very communicative upon these occasions. Should we send for her, she might scold us all out of the house.

Hastings. Let's see your list of the larder, then. I ask it as a favour. I always match my appetite to my bill of fare.

Marlow [*To* HARDCASTLE, *who looks at them with surprize*]. Sir, he's very right, and it's my way too.

Hardcastle. Sir, you have a right to command here. Here, Roger, bring us the bill of fare for to-night's supper. I believe it's drawn out. [*Exit* ROGER.] Your manner, Mr. Hastings, puts me in mind of my uncle, Colonel Wallop. It was a saying of his that no man was sure of his supper till he had eaten it.

Hastings [*Aside*]. All upon the high ropes! His uncle a colonel! We shall soon hear of his mother being a justice of peace. [*Re-enter* ROGER.] But let's hear the bill of fare.

Marlow [*Perusing*]. What's here? For the first course; for the second course; for the desert. The devil, sir, do you think we have brought down the whole Joiners Company, or the Corporation of Bedford,[50] to eat up such a supper? Two or three little things, clean and comfortable, will do.

Hastings. But let's hear it.

Marlow [*Reading*]. For the first course, at the top, a pig, and pruin sauce.

Hastings. Damn your pig, I say!

Marlow. And damn your pruin sauce, say I!

Hardcastle. And yet, gentlemen, to men that are hungry pig with pruin sauce is very good eating.

Marlow. At the bottom, a calve's tongue and brains.

Hastings. Let your brains be knock'd out, my good sir; I don't like them.

Marlow. Or you may clap them on a plate by themselves. I do.

Hardcastle [*Aside*]. Their impudence confounds me.

[50] It is suggested by a writer in *Notes and Queries*, May 16, 1903, that the corporation of Bedford, which was unusually large, was, like the Joiners' Company, notorious for its prowess at the table.

[*To them.*] Gentlemen, you are my guests, make what alterations you please. Is there any thing else you wish to retrench or alter, gentlemen?

Marlow. Item: a pork pie, a boiled rabbet and sausages, a florentine, a shaking pudding,[51] and a dish of tiff—taff —taffety cream![52]

Hastings. Confound your made dishes! I shall be as much at a loss in this house as at a green and yellow dinner at the French Ambassador's table. I'm for plain eating.

Hardcastle. I'm sorry, gentlemen, that I have nothing you like, but if there be any thing you have a particular fancy to—

Marlow. Why, really, sir, your bill of fare is so exquisite that any one part of it is full as good as another. Send us what you please. So much for supper. And now to see that our beds are air'd and properly taken care of.

Hardcastle. I entreat you'll leave all that to me. You shall not stir a step.

Marlow. Leave that to you! I protest, sir, you must excuse me, I always look to these things myself.

Hardcastle. I must insist, sir, you'll make yourself easy on that head.

Marlow [*Aside*]. You see I'm resolved on it.—A very troublesome fellow this, as ever I met with.

Hardcastle [*Aside*]. Well, sir, I'm resolved at least to attend you. This may be modern modesty, but I never saw any thing look so like old-fashioned impudence.

[*Exeunt* MARLOW *and* HARDCASTLE.

HASTINGS, *solus.*

Hastings. So I find this fellow's civilities begin to grow troublesome. But who can be angry at those assiduities which are meant to please him? Ha! what do I see? Miss Neville, by all that's happy!

Enter MISS NEVILLE.

Miss Neville. My dear Hastings! To what unexpected good fortune, to what accident, am I to ascribe this happy meeting?

Hastings. Rather let me ask the same question, as I

---

[51] A jelly or whitepot.

[52] Marlow stammers—cf. page 130, line 26. Taffety was a dish so called from its suggestion of the glossy silk known as taffeta or taffety.

could never have hoped to meet my dearest Constance at
an inn.

Miss Neville. An inn! Sure you mistake! My aunt, my
guardian, lives here. What could induce you to think this
house an inn?

Hastings. My friend, Mr. Marlow, with whom I came
down, and I, have been sent here as to an inn, I assure
you. A young fellow whom we accidentally met at a
house hard by directed us hither.

Miss Neville. Certainly it must be one of my hopeful
cousin's tricks, of whom you have heard me talk so often,
ha! ha! ha! ha!

Hastings. He whom your aunt intends for you? He
of whom I have such just apprehensions?

Miss Neville. You have nothing to fear from him, I
assure you. You'd adore him if you knew how heartily
he despises me. My aunt knows it too, and has undertaken
to court me for him, and actually begins to think she has
made a conquest.

Hastings. Thou dear dissembler! You must know, my
Constance, I have just seized this happy opportunity of
my friend's visit here to get admittance into the family.
The horses that carried us down are now fatigued with
their journey, but they'll soon be refreshed; and then,
if my dearest girl will trust in her faithful Hastings, we
shall soon be landed in France, where even among slaves
the laws of marriage[53] are respected.

Miss Neville. I have often told you, that though ready
to obey you, I yet should leave my little fortune behind
with reluctance. The greatest part of it was left me by
my uncle, the India Director, and chiefly consists in
jewels. I have been for some time persuading my aunt
to let me wear them. I fancy I'm very near succeeding.
The instant they are put into my possession you shall
find me ready to make them and myself yours.

Hastings. Perish the baubles! Your person is all I
desire. In the meantime, my friend Marlow must not be
let into his mistake. I know the strange reserve of his
temper is such that, if abruptly informed of it, he would

[53] This was an oblique reference to the marriage in 1766 of
the Duke of Gloucester and Lady Waldegrave, which helped
to bring about the Royal Marriage Act of 1772, directed at the
Royal Dukes.

instantly quit the house before our plan was ripe for execution.

Miss Neville. But how shall we keep him in the deception? Miss Hardcastle is just returned from walking; what if we still continue to deceive him?—This, this way—
                                                    [*They confer.*

Enter MARLOW.

Marlow. The assiduities of these good people teize me beyond bearing. My host seems to think it ill manners to leave me alone, and so he claps not only himself but his old-fashioned wife on my back. They talk of coming to sup with us, too; and then, I suppose, we are to run the gauntlet thro' all the rest of the family—What have we got here!—

Hastings. My dear Charles! Let me congratulate you!— The most fortunate accident! Who do you think is just alighted?

Marlow. Cannot guess.

Hastings. Our mistresses, boy, Miss Hardcastle and Miss Neville. Give me leave to introduce Miss Constance Neville to your acquaintance. Happening to dine in the neighbourhood, they called, on their return, to take fresh horses, here. Miss Hardcastle has just stept into the next room, and will be back in an instant. Wasn't it lucky? eh!

Marlow [*Aside*]. I have just been mortified enough of all conscience, and here comes something to complete my embarrassment.

Hastings. Well! but wasn't it the most fortunate thing in the world?

Marlow. Oh, yes! Very fortunate—a most joyful encounter—But our dresses, George, you know, are in disorder—What if we should postpone the happiness 'till tomorrow?—To-morrow at her own house—It will be every bit as convenient—And rather more respectful—To-morrow let it be.   [*Offering to go.*

Miss Neville. By no means, sir. Your ceremony will displease her. The disorder of your dress will shew the ardour of your impatience. Besides, she knows you are in the house, and will permit you to see her.

Marlow. O, the devil! how shall I support it? Hem! hem! Hastings, you must not go. You are to assist me, you know. I shall be confoundedly ridiculous. Yet, hang it, I'll take courage! Hem!

Hastings. Pshaw, man, it's but the first plunge, and all's over! She's but a woman, you know.

Marlow. And of all women she that I dread most to encounter!

Enter Miss Hardcastle, *as returned from walking, a bonnet, &c.*[54]

Hastings [*Introducing them*]. Miss Hardcastle, Mr. Marlow; I'm proud of bringing two persons of such merit together, that only want to know, to esteem each other.

Miss Hardcastle [*Aside*]. Now for meeting my modest gentleman with a demure face, and quite in his own manner. [*After a pause, in which he appears very uneasy and disconcerted.*] I'm glad of your safe arrival, sir—I'm told you had some accidents by the way.

Marlow. Only a few, madam. Yes, we had some. Yes, madam, a good many accidents, but should be sorry— madam—or rather glad of any accidents—that are so agreeably concluded. Hem!

Hastings [*To him*]. You never spoke better in your whole life. Keep it up, and I'll insure you the victory.

Miss Hardcastle. I'm afraid you flatter, sir. You that have seen so much of the finest company can find little entertainment in an obscure corner of the country.

Marlow [*Gathering courage*]. I have lived, indeed, in the world, madam; but I have kept very little company. I have been but an observer upon life, madam, while others were enjoying it.

Miss Neville. But that, I am told, is the way to enjoy it at last.

Hastings [*To him*]. Cicero never spoke better. Once more, and you are confirm'd in assurance for ever.

Marlow [*To him*]. Hem! Stand by me, then, and when I'm down, throw in a word or two to set me up again.

Miss Hardcastle. An observer, like you, upon life, were, I fear, disagreeably employed, since you must have had much more to censure than to approve.

Marlow. Pardon me, madam. I was always willing to

[54] The importance of this is shown by Miss Hardcastle's comment to Pimple (Act III.), "He never once looked up during the interview. Indeed, if he had, my bonnet would have kept him from seeing me."

be amused. The folly of most people is rather an object of mirth than uneasiness.

Hastings [*To him*]. Bravo, bravo. Never spoke so well in your whole life. Well, Miss Hardcastle, I see that you and Mr. Marlow are going to be very good company. I believe our being here will but embarrass the interview.

Marlow. Not in the least, Mr. Hastings. We like your company of all things. [*To him.*] Zounds, George! sure you won't go? How can you leave us?

Hastings. Our presence will but spoil conversation, so we'll retire to the next room. [*To him.*] You don't consider, man, that we are to manage a little *tête-à-tête* of our own.   [*Exeunt* HASTINGS *with* MISS NEVILLE.

Miss Hardcastle [*After a pause*]. But you have not been wholly an observer, I presume, sir. The ladies, I should hope, have employed some part of your addresses.

Marlow [*Relapsing into timidity*]. Pardon me, madam, I—I—I—as yet have studied—only—to—deserve them.

Miss Hardcastle. And that, some say, is the very worst way to obtain them.

Marlow. Perhaps so, madam. But I love to converse only with the more grave and sensible part of the sex—But I'm afraid I grow tiresome.

Miss Hardcastle. Not at all, sir; there is nothing I like so much as grave conversation myself: I could hear it for ever. Indeed, I have often been surprized how a man of *sentiment* could ever admire those light, airy pleasures, where nothing reaches the heart.

Marlow. It's—a disease—of the mind, madam. In the variety of tastes there must be some who, wanting a relish for—um-a-um.

Miss Hardcastle. I understand you, sir. There must be some, who, wanting a relish for refined pleasures, pretend to despise what they are incapable of tasting.

Marlow. My meaning, madam, but infinitely better expressed. And I can't help observing—a—

Miss Hardcastle [*Aside*]. Who could ever suppose this fellow impudent upon some occasions. [*To him.*] You were going to observe, sir—

Marlow. I was observing, madam—I protest, madam, I forget what I was going to observe.

Miss Hardcastle [*Aside*]. I vow and so do I. [*To him.*] You were observing, sir, that in this age of hypocrisy—something about hypocrisy, sir.

Marlow. Yes, madam. In this age of hypocrisy, there are few who upon strict enquiry do not—a—a—a—

Miss Hardcastle. I understand you perfectly, sir.

Marlow [Aside]. Egad, and that's more than I do myself!

Miss Hardcastle. You mean that in this hypocritical age there are few that do not condemn in public what they practise in private, and think they pay every debt to virtue when they praise it.

Marlow. True, madam; those who have most virtue in their mouths have least of it in their bosoms.[55] But I'm sure I tire you, madam.

Miss Hardcastle. Not in the least, sir; there's something so agreeable and spirited in your manner, such life and force—pray, sir, go on.

Marlow. Yes, madam. I was saying—that there are some occasions—when a total want of courage, madam, destroys all the—and puts us—upon a—a—a—

Miss Hardcastle. I agree with you entirely: a want of courage upon some occasions assumes the appearance of ignorance, and betrays us when we most want to excel. I beg you'll proceed.

Marlow. Yes, madam. Morally speaking, madam—but I see Miss Neville expecting us in the next room. I would not intrude for the world.

Miss Hardcastle. I protest, sir, I never was more agreeably entertained in all my life. Pray, go on.

Marlow. Yes, madam. I was—but she beckons us to join her. Madam, shall I do myself the honour to attend you?

Miss Hardcastle. Well, then, I'll follow.

Marlow [Aside]. This pretty smooth dialogue has done for me.   [*Exit.*

MISS HARDCASTLE, *sola.*

Miss Hardcastle. Ha! ha! ha! Was there ever such a sober, sentimental interview? [56] I'm certain he scarce look'd in my face the whole time. Yet the fellow, but for

---

[55] Cf. Voltaire's "La pudeur s'est enfuite des cœurs, et s'est refugié sur les lèvres" (Preface to Cantos VI., VII., and VIII. of Byron's *Don Juan*).

[56] This is no doubt aimed at the rival school of comedy. In Act III. Marlow finds Miss Hardcastle "sentimental."

his unaccountable bashfulness, is pretty well too. He has good sense, but then so buried in his fears that it fatigues one more than ignorance. If I could teach him a little confidence, it would be doing somebody that I know of a piece of service. But who is that somebody?—that, faith, is a question I can scarce answer.   [*Exit.*

Enter TONY *and* MISS NEVILLE, *followed by* MRS. HARDCASTLE *and* HASTINGS.

Tony. What do you follow me for, Cousin Con? I wonder you're not ashamed to be so very engaging.

Miss Neville. I hope, cousin, one may speak to one's own relations, and not be to blame.

Tony. Ay, but I know what sort of a relation you want to make me, though; but it won't do. I tell you, Cousin Con, it won't do; so I beg you'll keep your distance. I want no nearer relationship.

          [*She follows, coqueting him, to the back scene.*

Mrs. Hardcastle. Well! I vow, Mr. Hastings, you are very entertaining. There's nothing in the world I love to talk of so much as London, and the fashions, though I was never there myself.

Hastings. Never there! You amaze me! From your air and manner, I concluded you had been bred all your life either at Ranelagh, St. James's, or Tower Wharf.[57]

Mrs. Hardcastle. O, sir! you're only pleased to say so. We country persons can have no manner at all. I'm in love with the town, and that serves to raise me above some of our neighbouring rustics; but who can have a manner that has never seen the Pantheon, the Grotto Gardens, the Borough,[58] and such places where the nobility chiefly resort? All I can do is to enjoy London at second-hand. I take care to know every *tête-à-tête* from the *Scandalous Magazine,*[59] and have all the fashions as they come out, in

[57] Ranelagh Gardens were at Chelsea; St. James's parish was the fashionable quarter; Tower Wharf was in the vulgar City, next the Tower.

[58] The Pantheon was a concert room in Oxford Street; the Grotto Garden, at Clerkenwell; the Borough was in Southwark. There is ironic humour in this mingling of great and small in this and the foregoing note.

[59] *The Town and Country Magazine* at this time published *Tête-à-Tête* portraits with satirical biographies. Lamb refers to the pictures in his *Detached Thoughts on Books and Reading.*

a letter from the two Miss Rickets of Crooked-lane.[60] Pray how do you like this head, Mr. Hastings?

Hastings. Extremely elegant and *degagée*, upon my word, madam. Your friseur is a Frenchman, I suppose?

Mrs. Hardcastle. I protest, I dressed it myself from a print in the *Ladies Memorandum-book*[61] for the last year.

Hastings. Indeed. Such a head in a side-box,[62] at the Play-house, would draw as many gazers as my Lady May'ress at a City Ball.

Mrs. Hardcastle. I vow, since inoculation[63] began, there is no such thing to be seen as a plain woman; so one must dress a little particular or one may escape in the crowd.

Hastings. But that can never be your case, madam, in any dress! [*Bowing.*]

Mrs. Hardcastle. Yet, what signifies *my* dressing when I have such a piece of antiquity by my side as Mr. Hardcastle: all I can say will never argue down a single button from his cloaths. I have often wanted him to throw off his great flaxen wig, and where he was bald, to plaister it over, like my Lord Pately, with powder.

Hastings. You are right, madam: for, as among the ladies there are none ugly, so among the men there are none old.

Mrs. Hardcastle. But what do you think his answer was? Why, with his usual Gothic vivacity, he said I only wanted him to throw off his wig to convert it into a *tête* for my own wearing!

Hastings. Intolerable! At your age you may wear what you please, and it must become you.

Mrs. Hardcastle. Pray, Mr. Hastings, what do you take to be the most fashionable age about town?

Hastings. Some time ago forty was all the mode; but I'm told the ladies intend to bring up fifty for the ensuing winter.

Mrs. Hardcastle. Seriously? Then I shall be too young for the fashion!

Hastings. No lady begins now to put on jewels 'till she's past forty. For instance, miss there, in a polite circle,

[60] See note 12, *Good Natur'd Man*.
[61] An annual pocket-book and diary.
[62] See note 20, *Good Natur'd Man*.
[63] Inoculation dated from 1721; but its introduction was gradual.

would be considered as a child, as a mere maker of samplers.

Mrs. Hardcastle. And yet Mrs. Niece thinks herself as much a woman, and is as fond of jewels as the oldest of us all.

Hastings. Your niece, is she? And that young gentleman,—a brother of yours, I should presume?

Mrs. Hardcastle. My son, sir. They are contracted to each other. Observe their little sports. They fall in and out ten times a day, as if they were man and wife already. [*To them.*] Well, Tony, child, what soft things are you saying to your Cousin Constance, this evening?

Tony. I have been saying no soft things; but that it's very hard to be followed about so. Ecod! I've not a place in the house now that's left to myself but the stable.

Mrs. Hardcastle. Never mind him, Con, my dear. He's in another story behind your back.

Miss Neville. There's something generous in my cousin's manner. He falls out before faces to be forgiven in private.

Tony. That's a damned confounded—crack.

Mrs. Hardcastle. Ah, he's a sly one! Don't you think they're like each other about the mouth, Mr. Hastings? The Blenkinsop mouth to a T. They're of a size too. Back to back, my pretties, that Mr. Hastings may see you.[64] Come, Tony.

Tony. You had as good not make me, I tell you.

[*Measuring.*

Miss Neville. O lud! he has almost cracked my head.

Mrs. Hardcastle. O, the monster! For shame, Tony. You a man, and behave so!

Tony. If I'm a man, let me have my fortin. Ecod! I'll not be made a fool of no longer.

Mrs. Hardcastle. Is this, ungrateful boy, all that I'm to get for the pains I have taken in your education? I that have rock'd you in your cradle, and fed that pretty mouth with a spoon! Did not I work that waistcoat to make you genteel? Did not I prescribe for you every day, and weep while the receipt was operating?

Tony. Ecod! you had reason to weep, for you have been dosing me ever since I was born. I have gone through every receipt in the complete huswife ten times over; and

---

[64] Cf. *Vicar of Wakefield*, ch. XVI.

you have thoughts of coursing me through *Quincy* next spring. But, ecod! I tell you, I'll not be made a fool of no longer.

Mrs. Hardcastle. Wasn't it all for your good, viper? Wasn't it all for your good?

Tony. I wish you'd let me and my good alone, then. Snubbing this way when I'm in spirits. If I'm to have any good, let it come of itself; not to keep dinging it, dinging it into one so.

Mrs. Hardcastle. That's false; I never see you when you're in spirits. No, Tony, you then go to the ale house or kennel. I'm never to be delighted with your agreeable wild notes, unfeeling monster.

Tony. Ecod, Mamma, your own notes are the wildest of the two!

Mrs. Hardcastle. Was ever the like? But I see he wants to break my heart, I see he does.

Hastings. Dear madam, permit me to lecture the young gentleman a little. I'm certain I can persuade him to his duty.

Mrs. Hardcastle. Well! I must retire. Come Constance, my love. You see, Mr. Hastings, the wretchedness of my situation. Was ever poor woman so plagued with a dear, sweet, pretty, provoking, undutiful boy.

[*Exeunt* Mrs. Hardcastle *and* Miss Neville.

Hastings. Tony.

Tony [*Singing*]. *There was a young man riding by, and fain would have his will. Rang do didlo dee.* Don't mind her. Let her cry. It's the comfort of her heart. I have seen her and sister cry over a book for an hour together, and they said they liked the book the better the more it made them cry.

Hastings. Then you're no friend to the ladies, I find, my pretty young gentleman?

Tony. That's as I find 'um.

Hastings. Not to her of your mother's chusing, I dare answer? And yet she appears to me a pretty, well-tempered girl.

Tony. That's because you don't know her as well as I. Ecod! I know every inch about her; and there's not a more bitter, cantanckerous toad in all Christendom!

Hastings [*Aside*]. Pretty encouragement, this, for a lover!

Tony. I have seen her since the height of that. She has as many tricks as a hare in a thicket, or a colt the first day's breaking.

Hastings. To me she appears sensible and silent!

Tony. Ay, before company. But when she's with her play-mates, she's as loud as a hog in a gate.

Hastings. But there is a meek modesty about her that charms me.

Tony. Yes, but curb her never so little, she kicks up, and you're flung in a ditch.

Hastings. Well, but you must allow her a little beauty. —Yes, you must allow her some beauty.

Tony. Bandbox! She's all a made up thing, mun. Ah! could you but see Bet Bouncer of these parts, you might then talk of beauty. Ecod, she has two eyes as black as sloes, and cheeks as broad and red as a pulpit cushion. She'd make two of she.

Hastings. Well, what say you to a friend that would take this bitter bargain off your hands?

Tony. Anon.

Hastings. Would you thank him that would take Miss Neville, and leave you to happiness and your dear Betsy?

Tony. Ay; but where is there such a friend, for who would take *her?*

Hastings. I am he. If you but assist me, I'll engage to whip her off to France, and you shall never hear more of her.

Tony. Assist you! Ecod, I will, to the last drop of my blood. I'll clap a pair of horses to your chaise that shall trundle you off in a twinkling, and may be get you a part of her fortin besides, in jewels, that you little dream of.

Hastings. My dear Squire, this looks like a lad of spirit.

Tony. Come along then, and you shall see more of my spirit before you have done with me.   [*Singing.*

> *We are the boys*
> *That fears no noise*
> *Where the thundering cannons roar.*[65]

[*Exeunt.*

---

[65] O1, O2 print this like the rest of Tony's speech.

ACT III

SCENE—*The House*

Enter HARDCASTLE, *solus.*

HARDCASTLE. What could my old friend Sir Charles mean by recommending his son as the modestest young man in town? To me he appears the most impudent piece of brass that ever spoke with a tongue. He has taken possession of the easy chair by the fire-side already. He took off his boots in the parlour, and desired me to see them taken care of. I'm desirous to know how his impudence affects my daughter.—She will certainly be shocked at it.

Enter MISS HARDCASTLE, *plainly dressed.*

Hardcastle. Well, my Kate, I see you have changed your dress as I bid you; and yet, I believe, there was no great occasion.

Miss Hardcastle. I find such a pleasure, sir, in obeying your commands, that I take care to observe them without ever debating their propriety.

Hardcastle. And yet, Kate, I sometimes give you some cause, particularly when I recommended my *modest* gentleman to you as a lover to-day.

Miss Hardcastle. You taught me to expect something extraordinary, and I find the original exceeds the description!

Hardcastle. I was never so surprized in my life! He has quite confounded all my faculties!

Miss Hardcastle. I never saw any thing like it! And a man of the world, too!

Hardcastle. Ay, he learned it all abroad,—what a fool was I, to think a young man could learn modesty by travelling. He might as soon learn wit at a masquerade.

Miss Hardcastle. It seems all natural to him.

Hardcastle. A good deal assisted by bad company and a French dancing-master.

Miss Hardcastle. Sure, you mistake, papa! a French dancing-master could never have taught him that timid look,—that aukward address,—that bashful manner—

Hardcastle. Whose look, whose manner, child?

Miss Hardcastle. Mr. Marlow's: his *mauvaise honte*, his timidity struck me at the first sight.

Hardcastle. Then your first sight deceived you; for I think him one of the most brazen first sights that ever astonished my senses!

Miss Hardcastle. Sure, sir, you rally! I never saw any one so modest.

Hardcastle. And can you be serious! I never saw such a bouncing, swaggering puppy since I was born. Bully Dawson[66] was but a fool to him.

Miss Hardcastle. Surprising! He met me with a respectful bow, a stammering voice, and a look fixed on the ground.

Hardcastle. He met me with a loud voice, a lordly air, and a familiarity that made my blood freeze again.

Miss Hardcastle. He treated me with diffidence and respect; censured the manners of the age; admired the prudence of girls that never laughed; tired me with apologies for being tiresome; then left the room with a bow, and, "Madam, I would not for the world detain you."

Hardcastle. He spoke to me as if he knew me all his life before. Asked twenty questions, and never waited for an answer. Interrupted my best remarks with some silly pun, and when I was in my best story of the Duke of Marlborough and Prince Eugene, he asked if I had not a good hand at making punch. Yes, Kate, he ask'd your father if he was a maker of punch!

Miss Hardcastle. One of us must certainly be mistaken.

Hardcastle. If he be what he has shewn himself, I'm determined he shall never have my consent.

Miss Hardcastle. And if he be the sullen thing I take him, he shall never have mine.

Hardcastle. In one thing then we are agreed—to reject him.

Miss Hardcastle. Yes. But upon conditions. For if you should find him less impudent, and I more presuming; if you find him more respectful, and I more importunate— I don't know—the fellow is well enough for a man— Certainly we don't meet many such at a horse race in the country.

[66] A Whitefriars hector mentioned in *Spectator*, No. II.

Hardcastle. If we should find him so—But that's impossible. The first appearance has done my business. I'm seldom deceived in that.

Miss Hardcastle. And yet there may be many good qualities under that first appearance.

Hardcastle. Ay, when a girl finds a fellow's outside to her taste, she then sets about guessing the rest of his furniture. With her, a smooth face stands for good sense, and a genteel figure for every virtue.

Miss Hardcastle. I hope, sir, a conversation begun with a compliment to my good sense won't end with a sneer at my understanding?

Hardcastle. Pardon me, Kate. But if young Mr. Brazen can find the art of reconciling contradictions, he may please us both, perhaps.

Miss Hardcastle. And as one of us must be mistaken, what if we go to make further discoveries?

Hardcastle. Agreed. But depend on't I'm in the right.

Miss Hardcastle. And depend on't I'm not much in the wrong.   [*Exeunt.*

Enter TONY, *running in with a casket.*

Tony. Ecod! I have got them. Here they are. My Cousin Con's necklaces, bobs and all. My mother shan't cheat the poor souls out of their fortin[67] neither. O, my genus! is that you?

Enter HASTINGS.

Hastings. My dear friend, how have you managed with your mother? I hope you have amused her with pretending love for your cousin, and that you are willing to be reconciled at last? Our horses will be refreshed in a short time, and we shall soon be ready to set off.

Tony. And here's something to bear your charges by the way,—[*Giving the casket*] your sweetheart's jewels. Keep them, and hang those, I say, that would rob you of one of them!

Hastings. But how have you procured them from your mother?

Tony. Ask me no questions, and I'll tell you no fibs. I procured them by the rule of thumb. If I had not a key to every drawer in mother's bureau, how could I go to

[67] *fortin,* Octavos, fortune. But see p. 143, l. 32, p. 145, l. 31.

the alehouse so often as I do? An honest man may rob himself of his own at any time.

Hastings. Thousands do it every day. But to be plain with you; Miss Neville is endeavouring to procure them from her aunt this very instant. If she succeeds, it will be the most delicate way at least of obtaining them.

Tony. Well, keep them, till you know how it will be. But I know how it will be well enough; she'd as soon part with the only sound tooth in her head!

Hastings. But I dread the effects of her resentment when she finds she has lost them.

Tony. Never you mind her resentment, leave *me* to manage that. I don't value her resentment the bounce of a cracker. Zounds! here they are! Morrice, Prance!

[*Exit* HASTINGS.

TONY, MRS. HARDCASTLE, MISS NEVILLE.

Mrs. Hardcastle. Indeed, Constance, you amaze me. Such a girl as you want jewels? It will be time enough for jewels, my dear, twenty years hence, when your beauty begins to want repairs.

Miss Neville. But what will repair beauty at forty will certainly improve it at twenty, madam.

Mrs. Hardcastle. Yours, my dear, can admit of none. That natural blush is beyond a thousand ornaments. Besides, child, jewels are quite out at present. Don't you see half the ladies of our acquaintance, my Lady Kill-day-light, and Mrs. Crump, and the rest of them, carry their jewels to town, and bring nothing but paste and marcasites back?

Miss Neville. But who knows, madam, but somebody that shall be nameless would like me best with all my little finery about me?

Mrs. Hardcastle. Consult your glass, my dear, and then see, if with such a pair of eyes, you want any better sparklers. What do you think, Tony, my dear, does your Cousin Con want any jewels, in your eyes, to set off her beauty?

Tony. That's as thereafter may be.

Miss Neville. My dear aunt, if you knew how it would oblige me.

Mrs. Hardcastle. A parcel of old-fashioned rose and table-cut things.[68] They would make you look like the

---

[68] *I.e.* with flat surfaces.

court of King Solomon at a puppet-shew.[69] Besides, I believe I can't readily come at them. They may be missing,
for aught I know to the contrary.

Tony [*Apart to* MRS. HARDCASTLE]. Then why don't
you tell her so at once, as she's so longing for them. Tell
her they're lost. It's the only way to quiet her. Say they're
lost, and call me to bear witness.

Mrs. Hardcastle [*Apart to* TONY]. You know, my dear,
I'm only keeping them for you. So if I say they're gone,
you'll bear me witness, will you? He! he! he!

Tony [*Apart to* MRS. HARDCASTLE]. Never fear me.
Ecod! I'll say I saw them taken out with my own eyes.

Miss Neville. I desire them but for a day, madam. Just
to be permitted to shew them as relicks, and then they
may be lock'd up again.

Mrs. Hardcastle. To be plain with you, my dear Constance, if I could find them, you should have them. They're
missing, I assure you. Lost, for aught I know; but we
must have patience wherever they are.

Miss Neville. I'll not believe it; this is but a shallow
pretence to deny me. I know they're too valuable to be
so slightly kept, and as you are to answer for the loss.

Mrs. Hardcastle. Don't be alarm'd, Constance. If they
be lost, I must restore an equivalent. But my son knows
they are missing, and not to be found.

Tony. That I can bear witness to. They are missing,
and not to be found, I'll take my oath on't.

Mrs. Hardcastle. You must learn resignation, my dear;
for tho' we lose our fortune, yet we should not lose our
patience. See me, how calm I am.

Miss Neville. Ay, people are generally calm at the misfortunes of others.

Mrs. Hardcastle. Now, I wonder a girl of your good
sense should waste a thought upon such trumpery. We
shall soon find them; and, in the mean time, you shall make
use of my garnets till your jewels be found.

Miss Neville. I detest garnets!

Mrs. Hardcastle. The most becoming things in the
world to set off a clear complexion. You have often seen
how well they look upon me. You *shall* have them.
                                                    [*Exit*.

Miss Neville. I dislike them of all things. You shan't

---

[69] Goldsmith again refers to this Bartholomew Fair exhibition
in his Essay on the Coronation (*Essays*, 1776, 238).

stir.—Was ever any thing so provoking,—to mislay my own jewels, and force me to wear her trumpery.

Tony. Don't be a fool. If she gives you the garnets, take what you can get. The jewels are your own already. I have stolen them out of her bureau, and she does not know it. Fly to your spark, he'll tell you more of the matter. Leave me to manage *her.*

Miss Neville. My dear cousin!

Tony. Vanish. She's here, and has missed them already. [*Exit* MISS NEVILLE.] Zounds! how she fidgets and spits about like a Catherine wheel.

Enter MRS. HARDCASTLE.

Mrs. Hardcastle. Confusion! thieves! robbers! We are cheated, plundered, broke open, undone!

Tony. What's the matter, what's the matter, mamma? I hope nothing has happened to any of the good family!

Mrs. Hardcastle. We are robbed. My bureau has been broke open, the jewels taken out, and I'm undone!

Tony. Oh! is that all? Ha! ha! ha! By the laws, I never saw it better acted in my life. Ecod, I thought you was ruin'd in earnest, ha, ha, ha!

Mrs. Hardcastle. Why, boy, I *am* ruined in earnest. My bureau has been broke open, and all taken away.

Tony. Stick to that; ha, ha, ha! stick to that. I'll bear witness, you know, call me to bear witness.

Mrs. Hardcastle. I tell you, Tony, by all that's precious, the jewels are gone, and I shall be ruin'd for ever.

Tony. Sure I know they're gone, and I am to say so.

Mrs. Hardcastle. My dearest Tony, but hear me. They're gone, I say.

Tony. By the laws, mamma, you make me for to laugh, ha! ha! I know who took them well enough, ha! ha! ha!

Mrs. Hardcastle. Was there ever such a blockhead, that can't tell the difference between jest and earnest. I tell you I'm not in jest, booby!

Tony. That's right, that's right! You must be in a bitter passion, and then nobody will suspect either of us. I'll bear witness that they are gone.

Mrs. Hardcastle. Was there ever such a cross-grain'd brute, that won't hear me! Can you bear witness that you're no better than a fool? Was ever poor woman so beset with fools on one hand, and thieves on the other?

Tony. I can bear witness to that.

Mrs. Hardcastle. Bear witness again, you blockhead, you, and I'll turn you out of the room directly. My poor niece, what will become of *her!* Do you laugh, you unfeeling brute, as if you enjoy'd my distress?

Tony. I can bear witness to that.

Mrs. Hardcastle. Do you insult me, monster? I'll teach you to vex your mother, I will!

Tony. I can bear witness to that.

[*He runs off; she follows him.*

Enter Miss Hardcastle *and* Maid.

Miss Hardcastle. What an unaccountable creature is that brother of mine, to send them to the house as an inn, ha! ha! I don't wonder at his impudence.

Maid. But what is more, madam, the young gentleman as you passed by in your present dress, ask'd me if you were the bar maid? He mistook you for the bar maid, madam!

Miss Hardcastle. Did he? Then as I live I'm resolved to keep up the delusion. Tell me, Pimple, how do you like my present dress? Don't you think I look something like Cherry in the *Beaux' Stratagem*? [70]

Maid. It's the dress, madam, that every lady wears in the country, but when she visits or receives company.

Miss Hardcastle. And are you sure he does not remember my face or person?

Maid. Certain of it!

Miss Hardcastle. I vow, I thought so; for though we spoke for some time together, yet his fears were such that he never once looked up during the interview. Indeed, if he had, my bonnet would have kept him from seeing me.

Maid. But what do you hope from keeping him in his mistake?

Miss Hardcastle. In the first place, I shall be *seen*, and that is no small advantage to a girl who brings her face to market. Then I shall perhaps make an acquaintance, and that's no small victory gained over one who never addresses any but the wildest of her sex. But my chief aim is to take my gentleman off his guard, and like an invisible champion of romance examine the giant's force before I offer to combat.

Maid. But are you sure you can act your part, and dis-

[70] A comedy by George Farquhar, 1707. Cherry is the Lichfield inn-keeper's daughter of the piece.

guise your voice, so that he may mistake that, as he has already mistaken your person?

Miss Hardcastle. Never fear me. I think I have got the true bar cant.—Did your honour call?—Attend the Lion[71] there.—Pipes and tobacco for the Angel.—The Lamb has been outrageous this half hour!

Maid. It will do, madam. But he's here.   [*Exit* MAID.

Enter MARLOW.

Marlow. What a bawling in every part of the house; I have scarce a moment's repose. If I go to the best room, there I find my host and his story. If I fly to the gallery,[72] there we have my hostess with her curtesy down to the ground. I have at last got a moment to myself, and now for recollection.   [*Walks and muses.*

Miss Hardcastle. Did you call, sir? Did your honour call?

Marlow [*Musing*]. As for Miss Hardcastle, she's too grave and sentimental for me.

Miss Hardcastle. Did your honour call?

          [*She still places herself before him, he turning away.*

Marlow. No, child! [*Musing.*] Besides, from the glimpse I had of her, I think she squints.

Miss Hardcastle. I'm sure, sir, I heard the bell ring.

Marlow. No, no! [*Musing.*] I have pleased my father, however, by coming down, and I'll tomorrow please myself by returning.   [*Taking out his tablets, and perusing.*

Miss Hardcastle. Perhaps the other gentleman called, sir?

Marlow. I tell you no.

Miss Hardcastle. I should be glad to know, sir. We have such a parcel of servants.

Marlow. No, no, I tell you. [*Looks full in her face.*] Yes, child, I think I did call. I wanted—I wanted—I vow, child, you are vastly handsome!

Miss Hardcastle. O la, sir, you'll make one asham'd.

Marlow. Never saw a more sprightly, malicious eye. Yes, yes, my dear, I did call. Have you got any of your —a—what d'ye call it in the house?

---

[71] See note 58, *Good Natur'd Man.*

[72] The old inns had galleries round a central yard. Upon these the bedrooms opened. Mr. Hardcastle's house "looked for all the world like an inn."

Miss Hardcastle. No, sir, we have been out of that these ten days.

Marlow. One may call in this house, I find, to very little purpose. Suppose I should call for a taste, just by way of trial, of the nectar of your lips; perhaps I might be disappointed in that, too?

Miss Hardcastle. Nectar? nectar? that's a liquor there's no call for in these parts. French, I suppose. We keep no French wines here, sir.

Marlow. Of true English growth, I assure you.

Miss Hardcastle. Then it's odd I should not know it. We brew all sorts of wines in this house, and I have lived here these eighteen years.

Marlow. Eighteen years! Why one would think, child, you kept the bar before you were born. How old are you?

Miss Hardcastle. O! sir, I must not tell my age. They say women and music should never be dated.

Marlow. To guess at this distance, you can't be much above forty. [*Approaching.*] Yet nearer, I don't think so much. [*Approaching.*] By coming close to some women, they look younger still; but when we come very close indeed—   [*Attempting to kiss her.*

Miss Hardcastle. Pray, sir, keep your distance. One would think you wanted to know one's age as they do horses, by mark of mouth.

Marlow. I protest, child, you use me extremely ill. If you keep me at this distance, how is it possible you and I can be ever acquainted?

Miss Hardcastle. And who wants to be acquainted with you? I want no such acquaintance, not I. I'm sure you did not treat Miss Hardcastle that was here awhile ago in this obstropalous manner. I'll warrant me, before her you look'd dash'd, and kept bowing to the ground, and talk'd, for all the world, as if you was before a justice of peace.

Marlow [*Aside*]. Egad! she has hit it, sure enough. [*To her.*] In awe of her, child? Ha! ha! ha! A mere aukward, squinting thing! No, no! I find you don't know me. I laugh'd, and rallied her a little; but I was unwilling to be too severe. No, I could not be too severe, curse me!

Miss Hardcastle. O! then, sir, you are a favourite, I find, among the ladies?

Marlow. Yes, my dear, a great favourite. And yet, hang

me, I don't see what they find in me to follow. At the Ladies Club[73] in town I'm called their agreeable Rattle. Rattle, child, is not my real name, but one I'm known by. My name is Solomons. Mr. Solomons, my dear, at your service.   [*Offering to salute her.*

Miss Hardcastle. Hold, sir; you were introducing me to your club, not to yourself. And you're so great a favourite there you say?

Marlow. Yes, my dear. There's Mrs. Mantrap, Lady Betty Blackleg, the Countess of Sligo, Mrs. Longhorns, old Miss Biddy Buckskin,[74] and your humble servant, keep up the spirit of the place.

Miss Hardcastle. Then it's a very merry place, I suppose.

Marlow. Yes, as merry as cards, suppers, wine, and old women can make us.

Miss Hardcastle. And their agreeable Rattle, ha! ha! ha!

Marlow [*Aside*]. Egad! I don't quite like this chit. She looks knowing, methinks. You laugh, child!

Miss Hardcastle. I can't but laugh to think what time they all have for minding their work or their family.

Marlow [*Aside*]. All's well, she don't laugh at me. [*To her.*] Do *you* ever work, child?

Miss Hardcastle. Ay, sure. There's not a screen or a quilt in the whole house but what can bear witness to that.

Marlow. Odso! Then you must shew me your embroidery.[75] I embroider and draw patterns myself a little. If you want a judge of your work you must apply to me.
                                   [*Seizing her hand.*

Enter HARDCASTLE,[76] *who stands in surprize.*

Miss Hardcastle. Ay, but the colours don't look well by candle light. You shall see all in the morning.
                                          [*Struggling.*

[73] A so-called *Female Coterie* in Albemarle Street, described in the *Gentleman's Magazine* for 1770, pp. 414-15.

[74] This was supposed to be Miss Rachel Lloyd, a friend of Horace Walpole, and member of the Ladies' Club (Walpole to Lady Ossory, 27 March, 1773).

[75] Dr. Birkbeck Hill (*Boswell's Johnson*, 1887, v. 133) suggests that Goldsmith was here remembering the passage in Act IV. Sc. I of Farquhar's *Beaux' Stratagem*, where Archer says to Mrs. Sullen, "I can't at this distance, Madam, distinguish the figures of the embroidery."

[76] Placed in octavos after Marlow's exit; but see p. 156, l. 12.

Marlow. And why not now, my angel? Such beauty fires beyond the power of resistance.—Pshaw! the father here! My old luck: I never nick'd seven[77] that I did not throw ames-ace[78] three times following.   [*Exit* MARLOW.

Hardcastle. So, madam! So I find *this* is your *modest* lover. This is your humble admirer that kept his eyes fixed on the ground, and only ador'd at humble distance. Kate, Kate, art thou not asham'd to deceive your father so?

Miss Hardcastle. Never trust me, dear papa, but he's still the modest man I first took him for; you'll be convinced of it as well as I.

Hardcastle. By the hand of my body, I believe his impudence is infectious! Didn't I see him seize your hand? Didn't I see him hawl you about like a milk maid? And now you talk of his respect and his modesty, forsooth!

Miss Hardcastle. But if I shortly convince you of his modesty, that he has only the faults that will pass off with time, and the virtues that will improve with age, I hope you'll forgive him.

Hardcastle. The girl would actually make one run mad! I tell you I'll not be convinced. I am convinced. He has scarcely been three hours in the house, and he has already encroached on all my prerogatives. You may like his impudence, and call it modesty. But my son-in-law, madam, must have very different qualifications.

Miss Hardcastle. Sir, I ask but this night to convince you.

Hardcastle. You shall not have half the time, for I have thoughts of turning him out this very hour.

Miss Hardcastle. Give me that hour then, and I hope to satisfy you.

Hardcastle. Well, an hour let it be then. But I'll have no trifling with our father. All fair and open, do you mind me?

Miss Hardcastle. I hope, sir, you have ever found that I considered your commands as my pride; for your kindness is such that my duty as yet has been inclination.

[*Exeunt.*

[77] Seven was a lucky throw. To "nick it" was to be fortunate enough to make it.

[78] "Both aces,—the lowest throw upon the dice" (Dyce's *Glossary to Shakespeare*, by Littledale, 1902, p. 14).

ACT IV

SCENE—*The House*

Enter HASTINGS *and* MISS NEVILLE.

HASTINGS. You surprise me! Sir Charles Marlow expected here this night? Where have you had your information?

Miss Neville. You may depend upon it. I just saw his letter to Mr. Hardcastle, in which he tells him he intends setting out a few hours after his son.

Hastings. Then, my Constance, all must be completed before he arrives. He knows me; and should he find me here, would discover my name, and perhaps my designs, to the rest of the family.

Miss Neville. The jewels, I hope, are safe.

Hastings. Yes, yes. I have sent them to Marlow, who keeps the keys of our baggage. In the meantime, I'll go to prepare matters for our elopement. I have had the Squire's promise of a fresh pair of horses; and, if I should not see him again, will write him further directions. [*Exit.*

Miss Neville. Well, success attend you! In the meantime, I'll go amuse my aunt with the old pretence of a violent passion for my cousin.   [*Exit.*

Enter MARLOW, *followed by a* SERVANT.

Marlow. I wonder what Hastings could mean by sending me so valuable a thing as a casket to keep for him, when he knows the only place I have is the seat of a post-coach at an inn-door. Have you deposited the casket with the landlady, as I ordered you? Have you put it into her own hands?

Servant. Yes, your honour.

Marlow. She said she'd keep it safe, did she?

Servant. Yes, she said she'd keep it safe enough; she ask'd me how I came by it, and she said she had a great mind to make me give an account of myself.   [*Exit* SERVANT.

Marlow. Ha! Ha! Ha! They're safe, however. What an unaccountable set of beings have we got amongst! This little bar-maid, though, runs in my head most strangely, and drives out the absurdities of all the rest of the family. She's mine, she must be mine, or I'm greatly mistaken!

Enter HASTINGS.

Hastings. Bless me! I quite forgot to tell her that I intended to prepare at the bottom of the garden. Marlow here, and in spirits too!

Marlow. Give me joy, George! Crown me, shadow me with laurels! Well, George, after all, we modest fellows don't want for success among the women.

Hastings. Some women, you mean. But what success has your honour's modesty been crowned with now that it grows so insolent upon us?

Marlow. Didn't you see the tempting, brisk, lovely little thing that runs about the house with a bunch of keys to its girdle?

Hastings. Well! and what then?

Marlow. She's mine, you rogue, you. Such fire, such motion, such eyes, such lips—but egad! she would not let me kiss them though.

Hastings. But are you sure, so very sure of her?

Marlow. Why, man, she talk'd of shewing me her work above-stairs, and I am to improve[79] the pattern.

Hastings. But how can *you*, Charles, go about to rob a woman of her honour?

Marlow. Pshaw! pshaw! we all know the honour of the bar-maid of an inn. I don't intend to *rob* her, take my word for it;[80] there's nothing in this house, I shan't honestly *pay* for!

Hastings. I believe the girl has virtue.

Marlow. And if she has, I should be the last man in the world that would attempt to corrupt it.

Hastings. You have taken care, I hope, of the casket I sent you to lock up? It's in safety?

Marlow. Yes, yes. It's safe enough. I have taken care of it. But how could you think the seat of a post-coach at an inn-door a place of safety? Ah! numbskull! I have taken better precautions for you than you did for yourself.—I have—

Hastings. What!

Marlow. I have sent it to the landlady to keep for you.

Hastings. To the landlady!

Marlow. The landlady.

Hastings. You did!

---

[79] Percy's edition (1801, ii., 388) prints approve.
[80] The octavos have only a comma after "for it."

Marlow. I did. She's to be answerable for its forth-coming, you know.

Hastings. Yes, she'll bring it forth with a witness.

Marlow. Wasn't I right? I believe you'll allow that I acted prudently upon this occasion?

Hastings [*Aside*]. He must not see my uneasiness.

Marlow. You seem a little disconcerted, though, methinks. Sure nothing has happened?

Hastings. No, nothing. Never was in better spirits in all my life. And so you left it with the landlady, who, no doubt, very readily undertook the charge?

Marlow. Rather too readily. For she not only kept the casket, but, thro' her great precaution, was going to keep the messenger too. Ha! ha! ha!

Hastings. He! he! he! They're safe, however.

Marlow. As a guinea in a miser's purse.

Hastings [*Aside*]. So now all hopes of fortune are at an end, and we must set off without it. [*To him.*] Well, Charles, I'll leave you to your meditations on the pretty bar-maid, and, he! he! he! may you be as successful for yourself as you have been for me.   [*Exit.*

Marlow. Thank ye, George! I ask no more. Ha! ha! ha!

Enter HARDCASTLE.

Hardcastle. I no longer know my own house. It's turned all topsey-turvey. His servants have got drunk already. I'll bear it no longer,—and yet, from my respect for his father, I'll be calm. [*To him.*] Mr. Marlow, your servant. I'm your very humble servant.   [*Bowing low.*

Marlow [*Aside*]. Sir, your humble servant. What's to be the wonder now?

Hardcastle. I believe, sir, you must be sensible, sir, that no man alive ought to be more welcome than your father's son, sir. I hope you think so?

Marlow. I do, from my soul, sir. I don't want much intreaty. I generally make my father's son welcome wherever he goes.

Hardcastle. I believe you do, from my soul, sir. But tho' I say nothing to your own conduct, that of your servants is insufferable. Their manner of drinking is setting a very bad example in this house, I assure you.

Marlow. I protest, my very good sir, that's no fault of mine. If they don't drink as they ought, *they* are to blame. I ordered them not to spare the cellar; I did,

I assure you. [*To the side scene.*] Here let one of my servants come up. [*To him.*] My positive directions were, that as I did not drink myself, they should make up for my deficiencies below.

Hardcastle. Then they had your orders for what they do! I'm satisfied!

Marlow. They had, I assure you.[81] You shall hear from one of themselves.

Enter SERVANT, *drunk.*

Marlow. You, Jeremy! Come forward, sirrah! What were my orders? Were you not told to drink freely, and call for what you thought fit, for the good of the house?

Hardcastle [*Aside*]. I begin to lose my patience.

Jeremy. Please your honour, liberty and Fleet-street [82] for ever! Tho' I'm but a servant, I'm as good as another man. I'll drink for no man before supper, sir, dammy! Good liquor will sit upon a good supper, but a good supper will not sit upon—hiccup—upon my conscience, sir.   [*Exit* JEREMY.

Marlow. You see, my old friend, the fellow is as drunk as he can possibly be. I don't know what you'd have more, unless you'd have the poor devil soused in a beer-barrel.

Hardcastle. Zounds! He'll drive me distracted if I contain myself any longer. Mr. Marlow. Sir; I have submitted to your insolence for more than four hours, and I see no likelihood of its coming to an end. I'm now resolved to be master here, sir, and I desire that you and your drunken pack may leave my house directly.

Marlow. Leave your house!—Sure, you jest, my good friend! What, when I'm doing what I can to please you!

Hardcastle. I tell you, sir, you don't please me; so I desire you'll leave my house.

Marlow. Sure, you cannot be serious! At this time o' night, and such a night! You only mean to banter me?

Hardcastle. I tell you, sir, I'm serious; and, now that my passions are rouzed, I say this house is mine, sir; this house is mine, and I command you to leave it directly.

Marlow. Ha! ha! ha! A puddle in a storm. I shan't stir a step, I assure you. [*In a serious tone.*] This your house,

[81] O3 omits "you."

[82] Jeremy's cry is an obvious echo of the then popular "Wilkes and Liberty."

fellow! It's my house. This is my house. Mine, while I chuse to stay. What right have you to bid me leave this house, sir? I never met with such impudence, curse me, never in my whole life before!

Hardcastle. Nor I, confound me if ever I did! To come to my house, to call for what he likes, to turn me out of my own chair, to insult the family, to order his servants to get drunk, and then to tell me,—*This house is mine, sir.* But all that's impudent, it makes me laugh. Ha! ha! ha! Pray, sir, [*bantering*] as you take the house, what think you of taking the rest of the furniture? There's a pair of silver candlesticks, and there's a fire-screen, and here's a pair of brazen nosed bellows, perhaps you may take a fancy to them?

Marlow. Bring me your bill, sir, bring me your bill, and let's make no more words about it.

Hardcastle. There are a set of prints too. What think you of the *Rake's Progress*[83] for your own apartment?

Marlow. Bring me your bill, I say; and I'll leave you and your infernal house directly.

Hardcastle. Then there's a mahogony[84] table, that you may see your face in.

Marlow. My bill, I say.

Hardcastle. I had forgot the great chair, for your own particular slumbers, after a hearty meal.

Marlow. Zounds! Bring me my bill, I say, and let's hear no more on't.

Hardcastle. Young man, young man, from your father's letter to me, I was taught to expect a well-bred, modest man as a visitor here, but now I find him no better than a coxcomb and a bully; but he will be down here presently, and shall hear more of it. [*Exit.*

Marlow. How's this! Sure, I have not mistaken the house? Every thing looks like an inn. The servants cry "Coming." The attendance is aukward; the bar-maid, too, to attend us. But she's here, and will further inform me. Whither so fast, child? A word with you.

Enter MISS HARDCASTLE.

Miss Hardcastle [*Aside*]. Let it be short, then. I'm in a hurry.—I believe he begins to find out his mistake, but its too soon quite to undeceive him.

[83] Hogarth's engravings of 1735.
[84] *Mahogony*. Thus in all the octavos.

Marlow. Pray, child, answer me one question. What are you, and what may your business in this house be?

Miss Hardcastle. A relation of the family, sir.

Marlow. What! A poor relation?

Miss Hardcastle. Yes, sir. A poor relation appointed to keep the keys, and to see that the guests want nothing in my power to give them.

Marlow. That is, you act as the bar-maid of this inn.

Miss Hardcastle. Inn! O law!—What brought that in your head? One of the best families in the county keep an inn! Ha, ha, ha, old Mr. Hardcastle's house an inn!

Marlow. Mr. Hardcastle's house! Is this house Mr. Hardcastle's house, child?

Miss Hardcastle. Ay, sure. Whose else should it be?

Marlow. So then all's out, and I have been damnably imposed on. O, confound my stupid head, I shall be laugh'd at over the whole town. I shall be stuck up in caricatura in all the printshops. The Dullissimo Maccaroni.[85] To mistake this house of all others for an inn, and my father's old friend for an inn-keeper! What a swaggering puppy must he take me for! What a silly puppy do I find myself! There again, may I be hang'd, my dear, but I mistook you for the bar-maid!

Miss Hardcastle. Dear me! dear me! I'm sure there's nothing in my *behavour*[86] to put me upon a level with one of that stamp.

Marlow. Nothing, my dear, nothing. But I was in for a list of blunders, and could not help making you a subscriber. My stupidity saw every thing the wrong way. I mistook your assiduity for assurance, and your simplicity for allurement. But its over—this house I no more shew my *face* in!

Miss Hardcastle. I hope, sir, I have done nothing to disoblige you. I'm sure I should be sorry to affront any gentleman who has been so polite, and said so many civil things to me. I'm sure I should be sorry [*Pretending to cry.*] if he left the family upon my account. I'm sure I

[85] A reference to a series of satirical prints, then appearing at Darly's in the Strand and elsewhere, in which prominent personages were caricatured as *Macaronies*,—Macaroni being the current name for the dandies of the period.

[86] Modern editors print *behaviour*, but the persistence of the five octavos in thus spelling an italicised word warrants keeping it as an intentional mispronunciation of Miss Hardcastle.

should be sorry people said any thing amiss, since I have no fortune but my character.

Marlow [*Aside*]. By heaven, she weeps! This is the first mark of tenderness I ever had from a modest woman, and it touches me. [*To her.*] Excuse me, my lovely girl, you are the only part of the family I leave with reluctance. But to be plain with you, the difference of our birth, fortune and education, make an honourable connexion impossible; and I can never harbour a thought of seducing simplicity that trusted in my honour, or bringing ruin upon one whose only fault was being too lovely.

Miss Hardcastle [*Aside*]. Generous man! I now begin to admire him. [*To him.*] But I'm sure my family is as good as Miss Hardcastle's, and though I'm poor, that's no great misfortune to a contented mind, and, until this moment, I never thought that it was bad to want fortune.

Marlow. And why now, my pretty simplicity?

Miss Hardcastle. Because it puts me at a distance from one that if I had a thousand pound I would give it all to.

Marlow [*Aside*]. This simplicity bewitches me, so that if I stay I'm undone. I must make one bold effort, and leave her. [*To her.*] Your partiality in my favour, my dear, touches me most sensibly, and were I to live for myself alone, I could easily fix my choice. But I owe too much to the opinion of the world, too much to the authority of a father, so that—I can scarcely speak of it— it affects me! Farewell!   [*Exit.*

Miss Hardcastle. I never knew half his merit till now. He shall not go, if I have power or art to detain him. I'll still preserve the character in which I stoop'd to conquer, but will undeceive my papa, who, perhaps, may laugh him out of his resolution.   [*Exit.*

Enter TONY, MISS NEVILLE.

Tony. Ay, you may steal for yourselves the next time. I have done my duty. She has got the jewels again, that's a sure thing; but she believes it was all a mistake of the servants.

Miss Neville. But, my dear cousin, sure you won't forsake us in this distress. If she in the least suspects that I am going off, I shall certainly be locked up, or sent to my Aunt Pedigree's, which is ten times worse.

Tony. To be sure, aunts of all kinds are damn'd bad things. But what can I do? I have got you a pair of horses that will fly like Whistlejacket, and I'm sure you can't say but I have courted you nicely before her face. Here she comes; we must court a bit or two more, for fear she should suspect us. [*They retire, and seem to fondle.*

Enter MRS. HARDCASTLE.

Mrs. Hardcastle. Well, I was greatly fluttered, to be sure. But my son tells me it was all a mistake of the servants. I shan't be easy, however, till they are fairly married, and then let her keep her own fortune. But what do I see! Fondling together, as I'm alive! I never saw Tony so sprightly before. Ah, have I caught you, my pretty doves? What, billing, exchanging stolen glances, and broken murmurs! Ah!

Tony. As for murmurs, mother, we grumble a little now and then, to be sure. But there's no love lost between us.[87]

Mrs. Hardcastle. A mere sprinkling, Tony, upon the flame, only to make it burn brighter.

Miss Neville. Cousin Tony promises to give us more of his company at home. Indeed, he shan't leave us any more. It won't leave us, Cousin Tony, will it?

Tony. O, it's a pretty creature! No, I'd sooner leave my horse in a pound than leave you when you smile upon one so. Your laugh makes you so becoming.

Miss Neville. Agreeable cousin! Who can help admiring that natural humour, that pleasant, broad, red, thoughtless, [*Patting his cheek*]—ah, it's a bold face!

Mrs. Hardcastle. Pretty innocence!

Tony. I'm sure I always lov'd Cousin Con's hazle eyes, and her pretty long fingers, that she twists this way and that over the haspicholls, like a parcel of bobbins.

Mrs. Hardcastle. Ah, he would charm the bird from the tree. I was never so happy before. My boy takes after his father, Mr. Lumpkin, exactly. The jewels, my dear Con, shall be your's incontinently. You shall have them. Isn't he a sweet boy, my dear? You shall be married to-morrow, and we'll put off the rest of his education, like Dr. Drowsy's sermons, to a fitter opportunity.

Enter DIGGORY.

Diggory. Where's the 'Squire? I have got a letter for your worship.

[87] *I.e.* there has been no waste of affection on either side. Tony plays on the literal and the ironical use of this phrase.

Tony. Give it to my mamma. She reads all my letters first.

Diggory. I had orders to deliver it into your own hands.

Tony. Who does it come from?

Diggory. Your worship mun ask that o' the letter itself.
                                    [*Exit* DIGGORY.

Tony. I could wish to know, tho'.
                    [*Turning the letter, and gazing on it.*

Miss Neville [*Aside*]. Undone, undone! A letter to him from Hastings. I know the hand. If my aunt sees it, we are ruined for ever. I'll keep her employ'd a little if I can. [*To* MRS. HARDCASTLE.] But I have not told you, madam, of my cousin's smart answer just now to Mr. Marlow. We so laugh'd—You must know, madam—this way a little, for he must not hear us.   [*They confer.*

Tony [*Still gazing*]. A damn'd cramp piece of penmanship as ever I saw in my life. I can read your print-hand very well. But here there are such handles, and shanks, and dashes that one can scarce tell the head from the tail. *To Anthony Lumpkin, Esquire.* It's very odd, I can read the outside of my letters, where my own name is, well enough. But when I come to open it, it's all—buzz. That's hard, very hard; for the inside of the letter is always the cream of the correspondence.

Mrs. Hardcastle. Ha! ha! ha! Very well, very well. And so my son was too hard for the philosopher.

Miss Neville. Yes, madam; but you must hear the rest, madam. A little more this way, or he may hear us. You'll hear how he puzzled him again.

Mrs. Hardcastle. He seems strangely puzzled now himself, methinks.

Tony [*Still gazing*]. A damn'd up and down hand, as if it was disguised in liquor. [*Reading.*] *Dear Sir.* Ay that's that. Then there's an *M*, and a *T*, and an *S*, but whether the next be an izzard or an *R*, confound me, I cannot tell!

Mrs. Hardcastle. What's that, my dear? Can I give you any assistance?

Miss Neville. Pray, aunt, let me read it. No body reads a cramp hand better than I. [*Twitching the letter from her.*] Do you know who it is from?

Tony. Can't tell, except from Dick Ginger the feeder.

Miss Neville. Ay, so it is. [*Pretending to read.*]
"DEAR 'SQUIRE,

"Hoping that you're in health, as I am at this present. The gentlemen of the Shake-bag club[88] has cut the gentlemen of Goose-green quite out of feather. The odds—um—odd battle—um—long fighting—um, here, here, it's all about cocks, and fighting; it's of no consequence; here, put it up, put it up.

[*Thrusting the crumpled letter upon him.*

Tony. But, I tell you, miss, it's of all the consequence in the world! I would not lose the rest of it for a guinea! Here, mother, do you make it out. Of no consequence!

[*Giving* MRS. HARDCASTLE *the letter.*

Mrs. Hardcastle. How's this! [*Reads.*] "Dear 'Squire, I'm now waiting for Miss Neville, with a post-chaise and pair, at the bottom of the garden, but I find my horses yet unable to perform the journey. I expect you'll assist us with a pair of fresh horses, as you promised. Dispatch is necessary, as the *hag*, (ay, the hag) your mother, will otherwise suspect us. Yours, Hastings." Grant me patience. I shall run distracted! My rage choaks me!

Miss Neville. I hope, madam, you'll suspend your resentment for a few moments, and not impute to me any impertinence or sinister design that belongs to another.

Mrs. Hardcastle [*Curtesying very low*]. Fine spoken, madam; you are most miraculously polite and engaging, and quite the very pink of curtesy[89] and circumspection, madam. [*Changing her tone.*] And you, you great ill-fashioned oaf, with scarce sense enough to keep your mouth shut. Were you, too, join'd against me? But I'll defeat all your plots in a moment. As for you, madam, since you have got a pair of fresh horses ready, it would be cruel to disappoint them. So, if you please, instead of running away with your spark, prepare, this very moment, to run off with *me*. Your old Aunt Pedigree will keep you secure, I'll warrant me. You too, sir, may mount your horse, and guard us upon the way. Here, Thomas, Roger, Diggory! I'll shew you that I wish you better than you do yourselves.   [*Exit.*

Miss Neville. So now I'm completely ruined.

Tony. Ay, that's a sure thing.

Miss Neville. What better could be expected from being

---

[88] According to Halliwell, shake-bag is a large game-cock. (Cf. Smollett's *Humphrey Clinker*, I. 58.)

[89] *Romeo and Juliet*, Act II. Sc. 4. Cf. "Pink of perfection."

connected with such a stupid fool,—and after all the nods and signs I made him!

Tony. By the laws, miss, it was your own cleverness, and not my stupidity, that did your business. You were so nice and so busy with your Shake-bags and Goose-greens that I thought you could never be making believe.

Enter HASTINGS.

Hastings. So, sir, I find by my servant that you have shewn my letter and betray'd us. Was this well done, young gentleman?

Tony. Here's another. Ask miss there who betray'd you. Ecod, it was her doing; not mine.

Enter MARLOW.

Marlow. So I have been finely used here among you. Rendered contemptible, driven into ill manners, insulted, laugh'd at.

Tony. Here's another. We shall have old Bedlam broke loose presently.

Miss Neville. And there, sir, is the gentleman to whom we all owe every obligation.

Marlow. What can I say to him, a mere boy, an ideot, whose ignorance and age are a protection.

Hastings. A poor contemptible booby that would but disgrace correction.

Miss Neville. Yet with cunning and malice enough to make himself merry with all our embarrassments.

Hastings. An insensible cub.

Marlow. Replete with tricks and mischief.

Tony. Baw! damme, but I'll fight you both one after the other,—with baskets!

Marlow. As for him, he's below resentment. But your conduct, Mr. Hastings, requires an explanation. You knew of my mistakes, yet would not undeceive me.

Hastings. Tortured as I am with my own disappointments, is this a time for explanations? It is not friendly, Mr. Marlow.

Marlow. But, sir—

Miss Neville. Mr. Marlow, we never kept on your mistake, till it was too late to undeceive you. Be pacified.

Enter SERVANT.

Servant. My mistress desires you'll get ready immediately, madam. The horses are putting to. Your hat and things are in the next room. We are to go thirty miles before morning. [*Exit* SERVANT.

Miss Neville. Well, well; I'll come presently.

Marlow [*To* HASTINGS]. Was it well done, sir, to assist in rendering me ridiculous? To hang me out for the scorn of all my acquaintance? Depend upon it, sir, I shall expect an explanation.

Hastings. Was it well done, sir, if you're upon that subject, to deliver what I entrusted to yourself to the care of another, sir?

Miss Neville. Mr. Hastings. Mr. Marlow. Why will you increase my distress by this groundless dispute? I implore you—I intreat you—

Enter SERVANT.

Servant. Your cloak, madam. My mistress is impatient.

Miss Neville. I come. [*Exit* SERVANT.] Pray be pacified. If I leave you thus, I shall die with apprehension!

Enter SERVANT.

Servant. Your fan, muff, and gloves, madam. The horses are waiting.

Miss Neville. O, Mr. Marlow! if you knew what a scene of constraint and ill-nature lies before me, I'm sure it would convert your resentment into pity.

Marlow. I'm so distracted with a variety of passions that I don't know what I do. Forgive me, madam. George, forgive me. You know my hasty temper, and should not exasperate it.

Hastings. The torture of my situation is my only excuse.

Miss Neville. Well, my dear Hastings, if you have that esteem for me that I think, that I am sure you have, your constancy for three years will but encrease the happiness of our future connexion. If—

Mrs. Hardcastle [*Within*]. Miss Neville Constance, why, Constance, I say.

Miss Neville. I'm coming. Well, constancy. Remember, constancy is the word.   [*Exit, followed by the* SERVANT.

Hastings. My heart! How can I support this! To be so near happiness, and such happiness!

Marlow [*To* TONY]. You see now, young gentleman,

the effects of your folly. What might be amusement to
you is here disappointment, and even distress.

Tony [*From a reverie*]. Ecod, I have hit it. Its here. Your
hands. Your and yours, my poor Sulky. My boots there,
ho! Meet me two hours hence at the bottom of the
garden; and if you don't find Tony Lumpkin a more
good-natur'd fellow than you thought for, I'll give you
leave to take my best horse, and Bet Bouncer into the
bargain! Come along. My boots, ho! [*Exeunt.*

ACT V

SCENE I—*continues*

Enter HASTINGS *and* SERVANT.

HASTINGS. You saw the old lady and Miss Neville drive
off, you say?

Servant. Yes, your honour. They went off in a post
coach, and the young 'Squire went on horseback. They're
thirty miles off by this time.

Hastings. Then all my hopes are over.

Servant. Yes, sir. Old Sir Charles is arrived. He and
the old gentleman of the house have been laughing at
Mr. Marlow's mistake this half hour. They are coming
this way.

Hastings. Then I must not be seen. So now to my
fruitless appointment at the bottom of the garden. This is
about the time. [*Exit.*

Enter SIR CHARLES *and* HARDCASTLE.

Hardcastle. Ha! ha! ha! The peremptory tone in which
he sent forth his sublime commands.

Sir Charles. And the reserve with which I suppose he
treated all your advances.

Hardcastle. And yet he might have seen something in
me above a common inn-keeper too.

Sir Charles. Yes, Dick, but he mistook you for an uncommon innkeeper, ha! ha! ha!

Hardcastle. Well, I'm in too good spirits to think of any
thing but joy. Yes, my dear friend, this union of our
families will make our personal friendships hereditary:
and tho' my daughter's fortune is but small—

Sir Charles. Why, Dick, will you talk of fortune to *me?* My son is possessed of more than a competence already, and can want nothing but a good and virtuous girl to share his happiness and encrease it. If they like each other, as you say they do—

Hardcastle. If, man! I tell you they *do* like each other. My daughter as good as told me so.

Sir Charles. But girls are apt to flatter themselves, you know.

Hardcastle. I saw him grasp her hand in the warmest manner myself; and here he comes to put you out of your *ifs*, I warrant him.

Enter MARLOW.

Marlow. I come, sir, once more, to ask pardon for my strange conduct. I can scarce reflect on my insolence without confusion.

Hardcastle. Tut, boy, a trifle. You take it too gravely. An hour or two's laughing with my daughter will set all to rights again. She'll never like you the worse for it.

Marlow. Sir, I shall be always proud of her approbation.

Hardcastle. Approbation is but a cold word, Mr. Marlow; if I am not deceived, you have something more than approbation thereabouts. You take me.

Marlow. Really, sir, I have not that happiness.

Hardcastle. Come, boy, I'm an old fellow, and know what's what as well as you that are younger. I know what has past between you; but mum.

Marlow. Sure, sir, nothing has past between us but the most profound respect on my side, and the most distant reserve on hers. You don't think, sir, that my impudence has been past upon all the rest of the family?

Hardcastle. Impudence! No, I don't say that—Not quite impudence—Though girls like to be play'd with, and rumpled a little, too, sometimes. But she has told no tales, I assure you.

Marlow. I never gave her the slightest cause.

Hardcastle. Well, well, I like modesty in its place well enough. But this is over-acting, young gentleman. You *may* be open. Your father and I will like you the better for it.

Marlow. May I die, sir, if I ever—

Hardcastle. I tell you, she don't dislike you; and as I'm sure you like her—

Marlow. Dear sir—I protest, sir—

Hardcastle. I see no reason why you should not be joined as fast as the parson can tie you.

Marlow. But hear me, sir—

Hardcastle. Your father approves the match, I admire it, every moment's delay will be doing mischief, so—

Marlow. But why won't you hear me? By all that's just and true, I never gave Miss Hardcastle the slightest mark of my attachment, or even the most distant hint to suspect me of affection. We had but one interview, and that was formal, modest, and uninteresting.

Hardcastle [*Aside*]. This fellow's formal, modest impudence is beyond bearing.

Sir Charles. And you never grasp'd her hand, or made any protestations!

Marlow. As Heaven is my witness, I came down in obedience to your commands. I saw the lady without emotion, and parted without reluctance. I hope you'll exact no further proofs of my duty, nor prevent me from leaving a house in which I suffer so many mortifications.

[*Exit.*

Sir Charles. I'm astonish'd at the air of sincerity with which he parted.

Hardcastle. And I'm astonish'd at the deliberate intrepidity of his assurance.

Sir Charles. I dare pledge my life and honour upon his truth.

Hardcastle. Here comes my daughter, and I would stake my happiness upon her veracity.

Enter MISS HARDCASTLE.

Hardcastle. Kate, come hither, child. Answer us sincerely, and without reserve; has Mr. Marlow made you any professions of love and affection?

Miss Hardcastle. The question is very abrupt, sir! But since you require unreserved sincerity, I think he has.

Hardcastle [*To* SIR CHARLES]. You see.

Sir Charles. And pray, madam, have you and my son had more than one interview?

Miss Hardcastle. Yes, sir, several.

Hardcastle [*To* SIR CHARLES]. You see.

Sir Charles. But did he profess any attachment?

Miss Hardcastle. A lasting one.

Sir Charles. Did he talk of love?

Miss Hardcastle. Much, sir.

Sir Charles. Amazing. And all this formally?

Miss Hardcastle. Formally.

Hardcastle. Now, my friend, I hope you are satisfied.

Sir Charles. And how did he behave, madam?

Miss Hardcastle. As most profest admirers do. Said some civil things of my face, talked much of his want of merit, and the greatness of mine; mentioned his heart, gave a short tragedy speech, and ended with pretended rapture.

Sir Charles. Now I'm perfectly convinced, indeed. I know his conversation among women to be modest and submissive. This forward, canting, ranting manner by no means describes him, and I am confident he never sate for the picture.

Miss Hardcastle. Then what, sir, if I should convince you to your face of my sincerity? If you and my papa, in about half an hour, will place yourselves behind that screen, you shall hear him declare his passion to me in person.

Sir Charles. Agreed. And if I find him what you describe, all my happiness in him must have an end.   [*Exit*.

Miss Hardcastle. And if you don't find him what I describe—I fear my happiness must never have a beginning.   [*Exeunt*.

SCENE 2—*Changes to the back of the garden*

Enter HASTINGS.

HASTINGS. What an ideot am I, to wait here for a fellow who probably takes a delight in mortifying me. He never intended to be punctual and I'll wait no longer. What do I see? It is he, and perhaps with news of my Constance.

Enter TONY, *booted and spattered*.

Hastings. My honest 'Squire! I now find you a man of your word. This looks like friendship.

Tony. Ay, I'm your friend, and the best friend you have in the world, if you knew but all. This riding by night, by the bye, is cursedly tiresome. It has shook me worse than the basket of a stage-coach.

Hastings. But how? Where did you leave your fellow travellers? Are they in safety? Are they housed?

Tony. Five and twenty miles in two hours and a half is no such bad driving. The poor beasts have smoaked for it: rabbet me,[90] but I'd rather ride forty miles after a fox than ten with such *varment*.

Hastings. Well, but where have you left the ladies? I die with impatience.

Tony. Left them? Why, where should I leave them but where I found them?

Hastings. This is a riddle.

Tony. Riddle me this, then. What's that goes round the house, and round the house, and never touches the house?

Hastings. I'm still astray.

Tony. Why, that's it, mon. I have led them astray. By jingo, there's not a pond or slough within five miles of the place but they can tell the taste of.

Hastings. Ha, ha, ha, I understand; you took them in a round while they supposed themselves going forward. And so you have at last brought them home again.

Tony. You shall hear. I first took them down Feather-bed-lane, where we stuck fast in the mud. I then rattled them crack over the stones of Up-and-down Hill—I then introduc'd them to the gibbet on Heavy-tree Heath, and from that, with a circumbendibus,[91] I fairly lodged them in the horse-pond at the bottom of the garden.

Hastings. But no accident, I hope.

Tony. No, no. Only mother is confoundedly frightened. She thinks herself forty miles off.[92] She's sick of the journey, and the cattle can scarce crawl. So, if your own horses be ready, you may whip off with Cousin, and I'll be bound that no soul here can budge a foot to follow you.

Hastings. My dear friend, how can I be grateful?

Tony. Ay, now its "dear friend," "noble 'Squire." Just now, it was all "ideot," "cub," and run me through the guts. Damn *your* way of fighting, I say. After we take a knock in this part of the country, we kiss and be friends. But if you had run me through the guts, then I should be dead, and you might go kiss the hangman.

Hastings. The rebuke is just. But I must hasten to

[90] Fr. *rebattre*, to humble.

[91] A circuit. Dryden has this word in *The Spanish Friar*, 1681, Act v. Sc. 2.

[92] A trick of this kind was actually played by Sheridan on Mme. de Genlis (*Memoirs*, 1825, IV. 113-18).

relieve Miss Neville; if you keep the old lady employed, I promise to take care of the young one.

Tony. Never fear me. Here she comes. Vanish. [*Exit* Hastings].93 She's got from the pond, and draggled up to the waist like a mermaid.

Enter Mrs. Hardcastle.

Mrs. Hardcastle. Oh, Tony, I'm killed. Shook. Battered to death. I shall never survive it. That last jolt that laid us against the quickset hedge has done my business.

Tony. Alack, mama, it was all your own fault. You would be for running away by night, without knowing one inch of the way.

Mrs. Hardcastle. I wish we were at home again. I never met so many accidents in so short a journey. Drench'd in the mud, overturn'd in a ditch, stuck fast in a slough, jolted to a jelly, and at last to lose our way! Whereabouts do you think we are, Tony?

Tony. By my guess we should be upon Crackskull Common, about forty miles from home.

Mrs. Hardcastle. O lud! O lud! the most notorious spot in all the country. We only want a robbery to make a complete night on't.

Tony. Don't be afraid, mama, don't be afraid. Two of the five that kept here are hanged, and the other three may not find us. Don't be afraid. Is that a man that's galloping behind us? No; its only a tree. Don't be afraid.

Mrs. Hardcastle. The fright will certainly kill me.

Tony. Do you see any thing like a black hat moving behind the thicket?

Mrs. Hardcastle. Oh death!

Tony. No, it's only a cow. Don't be afraid, mama, don't be afraid.

Mrs. Hardcastle. As I'm alive, Tony, I see a man coming towards us. Ah! I'm sure on't. If he perceives us, we are undone.

Tony [*Aside*]. Father-in-law, by all that's unlucky, come to take one of his night walks. [*To her.*] Ah, it's a highwayman, with pistils as long as my arm. A damn'd ill-looking fellow.

Mrs. Hardcastle. Good Heaven defend us! He approaches.

93 [*Exit Hastings.*] The octavos place this after "young one."

Tony. Do you hide yourself in that thicket, and leave me to manage him. If there be any danger, I'll cough and cry hem. When I cough be sure to keep close.

[MRS. HARDCASTLE *hides behind a tree in the back scene.*

Enter HARDCASTLE.

Hardcastle. I'm mistaken, or I heard voices of people in want of help. Oh, Tony, is that you? I did not expect you so soon back. Are your mother and her charge in safety?

Tony. Very safe, sir, at my Aunt Pedigree's. Hem.

Mrs. Hardcastle [*From behind*]. Ah, death! I find there's danger.

Hardcastle. Forty miles in three hours; sure that's too much, my youngster.

Tony. Stout horses and willing minds make short journies, as they say. Hem.

Mrs. Hardcastle [*From behind*]. Sure he'll do the dear boy no harm.

Hardcastle. But I heard a voice here; I should be glad to know from whence it came?

Tony. It was I, sir, talking to myself, sir. I was saying that forty miles in four hours was very good going. Hem. As to be sure it was. Hem. I have got a sort of cold by being out in the air. We'll go in, if you please. Hem.

Hardcastle. But if you talk'd to yourself, you did not answer yourself. I am certain I heard two voices, and am resolved [*raising his voice*] to find the other out.

Mrs. Hardcastle [*From behind*]. Oh, he's coming to find me out! Oh!

Tony. What need you go, sir, if I tell you? Hem. I'll lay down my life for the truth[94]—hem—I'll tell you all, sir.   [*Detaining him.*

Hardcastle. I tell you I will not be detained. I insist on seeing. It's in vain to expect I'll believe you.

Mrs. Hardcastle [*Running forward from behind*]. O lud, he'll murder my poor boy, my darling. Here, good gentleman, whet your rage upon me. Take my money, my life, but spare that young gentleman, spare my child, if you have any mercy.

Hardcastle. My wife, as I'm a Christian! From whence can she come, or what does she mean?

[94] This was the motto of Jean Jacques Rousseau.

Mrs. Hardcastle [*Kneeling*]. Take compassion on us, good Mr. Highwayman. Take our money, our watches, all we have, but spare our lives. We will never bring you to justice, indeed we won't, good Mr. Highwayman.

Hardcastle. I believe the woman's out of her senses. What, Dorothy, don't you know *me?*

Mrs. Hardcastle. Mr. Hardcastle, as I'm alive! My fears blinded me. But, who, my dear, could have expected to meet you here, in this frightful place, so far from home. What has brought you to follow us?

Hardcastle. Sure, Dorothy, you have not lost your wits! So far from home, when you are within forty yards of your own door! [*To him.*] This is one of your old tricks, you graceless rogue, you! [*To her.*] Don't you know the gate, and the mulberry-tree; and don't you remember the horsepond, my dear?

Mrs. Hardcastle. Yes, I shall remember the horsepond as long as I live; I have caught my death in it. [*To* TONY.] And is it to you, you graceless varlet, I owe all this? I'll teach you to abuse your mother, I will.

Tony. Ecod, mother, all the parish says you have spoil'd me, and so you may take the fruits on't.

Mrs. Hardcastle. I'll spoil you, I will.

[*Follows him off the stage. Exit.*

Hardcastle. There's morality, however, in his reply.

[*Exit.*

Enter HASTINGS *and* MISS NEVILLE.

Hastings. My dear Constance, why will you deliberate thus? If we delay a moment, all is lost for ever. Pluck up a little resolution, and we shall soon be out of the reach of her malignity.

Miss Neville. I find it impossible. My spirits are so sunk with the agitations I have suffered that I am unable to face any new danger. Two or three years patience will at last crown us with happiness.

Hastings. Such a tedious delay is worse than inconstancy. Let us fly, my charmer. Let us date our happiness from this very moment. Perish fortune. Love and content will encrease what we possess beyond a monarch's revenue. Let me prevail.

Miss Neville. No, Mr. Hastings, no. Prudence once more comes to my relief, and I will obey its dictates. In the moment of passion, fortune may be despised, but it ever produces a lasting repentance. I'm resolved to apply to Mr. Hardcastle's compassion and justice for redress.

Hastings. But tho' he had had the will, he has not the power to relieve you.

Miss Neville. But he has influence, and upon that I am resolved to rely.

Hastings. I have no hopes. But since you persist, I must reluctantly obey you.   [*Exeunt.*

SCENE 3—*Changes to a room at* MR. HARDCASTLE'S

Enter SIR CHARLES *and* MISS HARDCASTLE.

SIR CHARLES. What a situation am I in! If what you say appears, I shall then find a guilty son. If what he says be true, I shall then lose one that, of all others, I most wish'd for a daughter.

Miss Hardcastle. I am proud of your approbation; and, to shew I merit it, if you place yourselves as I directed, you shall hear his explicit declaration. But he comes.

Sir Charles. I'll to your father, and keep him to the appointment.   [*Exit* SIR CHARLES.

Enter MARLOW.

Marlow. Tho' prepar'd for setting out, I come once more to take leave, nor did I, till this moment, know the pain I feel in the separation.

Miss Hardcastle [*In her own natural manner*]. I believe these sufferings cannot be very great, sir, which you can so easily remove. A day or two longer, perhaps, might lessen your uneasiness, by shewing the little value of what you now think proper to regret.

Marlow [*Aside*]. This girl every moment improves upon me. [*To her.*] It must not be, madam. I have already trifled too long with my heart. My very pride begins to submit to my passion. The disparity of education and fortune, the anger of a parent, and the contempt of my equals begin to lose their weight, and nothing can restore me to myself but this painful effort of resolution.

Miss Hardcastle. Then go, sir. I'll urge nothing more to detain you. Tho' my family be as good as her's you came down to visit, and my education, I hope, not inferior, what are these advantages without equal affluence? I must remain contented with the slight approbation of imputed merit; I must have only the mockery of your addresses, while all your serious aims are fix'd on fortune.

Enter HARDCASTLE *and* SIR CHARLES *from behind.*

Sir Charles. Here, behind this screen.

Hardcastle. Ay, ay, make no noise. I'll engage my Kate covers him with confusion at last.

Marlow. By heavens, madam, fortune was ever my smallest consideration. Your beauty at first caught my eye; for who could see that without emotion? But every moment that I converse with you steals in some new grace, heightens the picture, and gives it stronger expression. What at first seem'd rustic plainness, now appears refin'd simplicity. What seem'd forward assurance, now strikes me as the result of courageous innocence and conscious virtue.

Sir Charles. What can it mean? He amazes me!

Hardcastle. I told you how it would be. Hush!

Marlow. I am now determined to stay, madam, and I have too good an opinion of my father's discernment, when he sees you, to doubt his approbation.

Miss Hardcastle. No, Mr. Marlow, I will not, cannot detain you. Do you think I could suffer a connexion in which there is the smallest room for repentance? Do you think I would take the mean advantage of a transient passion to load you with confusion? Do you think I could ever relish that happiness which was acquired by lessening your's?

Marlow. By all that's good, I can have no happiness but what's in your power to grant me. Nor shall I ever feel repentance but in not having seen your merits before. I will stay, even contrary to your wishes; and tho' you should persist to shun me, I will make my respectful assiduities atone for the levity of my past conduct.

Miss Hardcastle. Sir, I must entreat you'll desist. As our acquaintance began, so let it end, in indifference. I might have given an hour or two to levity; but, seriously, Mr. Marlow, do you think I could ever submit to a connexion where *I* must appear mercenary and *you* imprudent? Do you think I could ever catch at the confident addresses of a secure admirer?

Marlow [*Kneeling*]. Does this look like security? Does this look like confidence? No, madam, every moment that shews me your merit only serves to encrease my diffidence and confusion. Here let me continue—

Sir Charles. I can hold it no longer. Charles, Charles, how hast thou deceived me! Is this your indifference, your uninteresting conversation!

Hardcastle. Your cold contempt! your formal interview! What have you to say now?

Marlow. That I'm all amazement? What can it mean?

Hardcastle. It means that you can say and unsay things at pleasure. That you can address a lady in private, and deny it in public; that you have one story for us, and another for my daughter!

Marlow. Daughter!—this lady, your daughter!

Hardcastle. Yes, sir, my only daughter. My Kate, whose else should she be?

Marlow. Oh, the devil!

Miss Hardcastle. Yes, sir, that very identical tall, squinting lady you were pleased to take me for. [*Curtesying.*] She that you addressed as the mild, modest, sentimental man of gravity, and the bold, forward, agreeable Rattle of the Ladies Club; ha, ha, ha!

Marlow. Zounds, there's no bearing this; it's worse than death!

Miss Hardcastle. In which of your characters, sir, will you give us leave to address you? As the faultering gentleman, with looks on the ground, that speaks just to be heard, and hates hypocrisy: or the loud, confident creature that keeps it up with Mrs. Mantrap and old Miss Biddy Buckskin till three in the morning; ha, ha, ha!

Marlow. O, curse on my noisy head. I never attempted to be impudent yet that I was not taken down. I must be gone.

Hardcastle. By the hand of my body, but you shall not. I see it was all a mistake, and I am rejoiced to find it. You shall not, sir, I tell you. I know she'll forgive you. Won't you forgive him, Kate? We'll all forgive you. Take courage, man.   [*They retire, she tormenting him, to the back scene.*]

Enter MRS. HARDCASTLE, TONY.

Mrs. Hardcastle. So, so, they're gone off. Let them go. I care not.

Hardcastle. Who gone?

Mrs. Hardcastle. My dutiful niece and her gentleman, Mr. Hastings, from town. He who came down with our modest visitor, here.

Sir Charles. Who, my honest George Hastings? As worthy a fellow as lives, and the girl could not have made a more prudent choice.

Hardcastle. Then, by the hand of my body, I'm proud of the connexion.

Mrs. Hardcastle. Well, if he has taken away the lady, he has not taken her fortune; that remains in this family to console us for her loss.

Hardcastle. Sure, Dorothy, you would not be so mercenary?

Mrs. Hardcastle. Ay, that's my affair, not your's.

[*Hardcastle.*] But, you know, if your son, when of age, refuses to marry his cousin, her whole fortune is then at her own disposal.

[*Mrs.*] *Hardcastle.* Ay, but he's not of age, and she has not thought proper to wait for his refusal.⁹⁵

Enter HASTINGS *and* MISS NEVILLE.

Mrs. Hardcastle [*Aside*]. What! returned so soon? I begin not to like it.

Hastings [*To* HARDCASTLE]. For my late attempt to fly off with your niece, let my present confusion be my punishment. We are now come back, to appeal from your justice to your humanity. By her father's consent, I first paid her my addresses, and our passions were first founded in duty.

Miss Neville. Since his death, I have been obliged to stoop to dissimulation to avoid oppression. In an hour of levity, I was ready even to give up my fortune to secure my choice. But I'm now recover'd from the delusion, and hope from your tenderness what is denied me from a nearer connexion.

Mrs. Hardcastle. Pshaw, pshaw, this is all but the whining end of a modern novel!

Hardcastle. Be it what it will, I'm glad they're come back to reclaim their due. Come hither, Tony, boy. Do you refuse this lady's hand whom I now offer you?

Tony. What signifies my refusing? You know I can't refuse her till I'm of age, father.

⁹⁵ The octavos give Mrs. Hardcastle *But . . . disposal,* and Hardcastle, *Ay, . . . refusal.* Correct in Prior's ed. 1837.

Hardcastle. While I thought concealing your age, boy, was likely to conduce to your improvement, I concurred with your mother's desire to keep it secret. But since I find she turns it to a wrong use, I must now declare, you have been of age these three months.

Tony. Of age! Am I of age, father?

Hardcastle. Above three months.

Tony. Then you'll see the first use I'll make of my liberty. [*Taking* Miss Neville's *hand.*] Witness all men by these presents, that I, Anthony Lumpkin, Esquire, of BLANK place, refuse you, Constantia Neville, spinster, of no place at all, for my true and lawful wife. So Constance Neville may marry whom she pleases,[96] and Tony Lumpkin is his own man again!

Sir Charles. O brave 'Squire!

Hastings. My worthy friend!

Mrs. Hardcastle. My undutiful offspring!

Marlow. Joy, my dear George, I give you joy sincerely. And could I prevail upon my little tyrant here to be less arbitrary, I should be the happiest man alive, if you would return me the favour.

Hastings [*To* Miss Hardcastle]. Come, madam, you are now driven to the very last scene of all your contrivances. I know you like him, I'm sure he loves you, and you must and shall have him.

Hardcastle [*Joining their hands*]. And I say so too. And Mr. Marlow, if she makes as good a wife as she has a daughter, I don't believe you'll ever repent your bargain. So now to supper; to-morrow we shall gather all the poor of the parish about us, and the Mistakes of the Night shall be crowned with a merry morning; so boy, take her; and as you have been mistaken in the mistress, my wish is that you may never be mistaken in the wife.

[96] The usual stage variant, "may go to the devil," has no warrant from the octavos.

EPILOGUE [97]

BY DR. GOLDSMITH

WELL, having stoop'd to conquer with success,
And gain'd a husband without aid from dress,
Still as a bar-maid, I could wish it, too,
As I have conquer'd him to conquer you:
And let me say, for all your resolution,
That pretty bar-maids have done execution.
Our life is all a play, compos'd to please,
"We have our exits and our entrances." [98]
The first act shews the simple country maid,
Harmless and young, of ev'ry thing afraid,
Blushes when hir'd, and with unmeaning action,
I hopes as how to give you satisfaction.
Her second act displays a livelier scene,—
Th' unblushing bar-maid of a country inn.
Who whisks about the house, at market caters,
Talks loud, coquets the guests, and scolds the waiters.
Next the scene shifts to town, and there she soars,
The chop-house toast of ogling connoissieurs.
On 'Squires and Cits she there displays her arts,
And on the gridiron broils her lovers' hearts—
And as she smiles, her triumphs to compleat,
Even Common Councilmen forget to eat.
The fourth act shews her wedded to the 'Squire,
And Madam now begins to hold it higher;
Pretends to taste, at Operas cries *caro*,
And quits her *Nancy Dawson*,[99] for *Che Faro*.[100]
Doats upon dancing, and in all her pride,
Swims round the room, the *Heinel* of Cheapside:
Ogles and leers with artificial skill,
Till having lost in age the power to kill,
She sits all night at cards, and ogles at spadille.
Such, thro' our lives, the eventful history—
The fifth and last act still remains for me.
The Bar-maid now for your protection prays,
Turns female barrister, and pleads for Bayes.

[97] In the octavos this follows Garrick's Prologue. This was spoken by Mrs. Bulkley as Miss Hardcastle.

[98] *As You Like It*, Act II. Sc. 7.

[99] A song taking its name from a famous horn-pipe dancer and "toast," who died at Hampstead in 1767.

[100] "*Che faro senza Euridice*" in Glück's opera of *Orfeo*, 1764.

EPILOGUE [101]

To be spoken in the character of TONY LUMPKIN

BY J. CRADDOCK, ESQ.[102]

WELL—now all's ended—and my comrades gone,
Pray what becomes of *mother's nonly son?*
A hopeful blade!—in town I'll fix my station,
And try to make a bluster in the nation.
As for my cousin Neville, I renounce her,
Off—in a crack—I'll carry big Bett Bouncer.
 Why should not I in the great world appear?
I soon shall have a thousand pounds a year;
No matter what a man may here inherit,
In London—'gad, they've some regard to[103] spirit.
 I see the horses prancing up the streets,
And big Bet Bouncer bobs to all she meets;
Then hoikes to jiggs and pastimes ev'ry night—
Not to the plays—they say it a'n't polite;
To Sadler's-Wells[104] perhaps, or operas go,
And once, by chance, to the roratorio.
Thus here and there, for ever up and down,
We'll set the fashions, too, to half the town;
And then at auctions—money ne'er regard,
Buy pictures like the great, ten pounds a yard:
Zounds, we shall make these London gentry say,
We know what's damn'd genteel, as well as they.

[101] In O1 this is placed before the play, following Goldsmith's own epilogue. This came to late to be spoken.
[102] J. Craddock, Esq., of Gumley, in Leicestershire, a friend of Goldsmith's latter days. Craddock wrote a tragedy of *Zobeide*, 1771, translated from *Les Scythes* of Voltaire, and *Memoirs*, 1826-8.
[103] Some recent editions print, regard for.
[104] A pleasure garden near the New River Head at Islington.

EPILOGUE [105]

"MY DEAR SIR,

The Play [*She Stoops to Conquer*] has met with a success much beyond your expectations or mine. I thank you sincerely for your Epilogue, which, however could not be used, but with your permission, shall be printed.[106] The story in short is this; Murphy sent me rather the outline of an Epilogue than an Epilogue, which was to be sung by Mrs. Catley, and which she approved. Mrs. Bulkley hearing this, insisted on throwing up her part, unless according to the custom of the theatre, she were permitted to speak the Epilogue. In this embarrassment I thought of making a quarrelling Epilogue between Catley and her, debating who should speak the Epilogue, but then Mrs. Catley refused, after I had taken the trouble of drawing it out. I was then at a loss indeed; an Epilogue was to be made, and for none but Mrs. Bulkley. I made one, and Colman thought it too bad to be spoken; I was obliged therefore to try a fourth time, and I made a very mawkish thing, as you'll shortly see. Such is the history of my Stage adventures, and which I have at last done with. I cannot help saying that I am very sick of the stage; and though I believe I shall get three tolerable benefits, yet I shall upon the whole be a loser, even in a pecuniary light; my ease and comfort I certainly lost while it was in agitation.

I am, my dear Cradock,

your obliged, and obedient servant,

OLIVER GOLDSMITH.

P.S.—Present my most humble respects to Mrs. Cradock."

INTENDED TO HAVE BEEN SPOKEN BY MRS. BULKLEY AND MISS CATLEY FOR "SHE STOOPS TO CONQUER."

Enter MRS. BULKLEY, *who curtsies very low as beginning to speak. Then enter* MISS CATLEY, *who stands full before her, and curtsies to the audience.*

MRS. BULKLEY.

HOLD, Ma'am, your pardon. What's your business here?

---

[105] This, first printed in Percy's *Miscellaneous Works* of Goldsmith, 1801, ii. 82-86, is evidently the "quarrelling Epilogue" referred to in the following letter from Goldsmith to Joseph Craddock of Gumley (*Miscellaneous Memoirs*, 1826, i. 225-226).

[106] See Goldsmith's note, p. 183.

MISS CATLEY.

The Epilogue.

MRS. BULKLEY.

The Epilogue?

MISS CATLEY.

Yes, the Epilogue, my dear.

MRS. BULKLEY.

Sure you mistake, Ma'am. The Epilogue, *I* bring it.

MISS CATLEY.

Excuse me, Ma'am. The Author bid *me* sing it.

Recitative.

Ye beaux and belles, that form this splendid ring,
Suspend your conversation while I sing.

MRS. BULKLEY.

Why, sure the girl's beside herself: an Epilogue of singing,
A hopeful end indeed to such a blest beginning.
Besides, a singer in a comic set!—
Excuse me, Ma'am, I know the etiquette.

MISS CATLEY.

What if we leave it to the House?

MRS. BULKLEY.

The House!—Agreed.

MISS CATLEY.

Agreed.

MRS. BULKLEY.

And she, whose party's largest, shall proceed.
And first, I hope you'll readily agree
I've all the critics and the wits for me.
They, I am sure, will answer my commands;
Ye candid judging few, hold up your hands.
What! no return? I find too late, I fear,
That modern judges seldom enter here.

MISS CATLEY.

I'm for a different set.—Old men, whose trade is
Still to gallant and dangle with the ladies;—

Recitative.

Who mump their passion, and who, grimly smiling,
Still thus address the fair with voice beguiling:—

Air—Cotillion.

Turn, my fairest, turn, if ever
   Strephon caught thy ravish'd eye;
Pity take on your swain so clever,
   Who without your aid must die.
      Yes, I shall die, hu, hu, hu, hu!
      Yes, I must die, ho, ho, ho, ho!
                 (*Da capo.*)

MRS. BULKLEY.

Let all the old pay homage to your merit;
Give me the young, the gay, the men of spirit.
Ye travell'd tribe, ye macaroni train,
Of French friseurs, and nosegays, justly vain,
Who take a trip to Paris once a year
To dress, and look like awkward Frenchmen here,
Lend me your hands.—Oh! fatal news to tell:
Their hands are only lent to the Heinel.

MISS CATLEY.

Ay, take your travellers, travellers indeed!
Give me my bonny Scot, that travels from the Tweed.
Where are the chiels? Ah! Ah, I well discern
The smiling looks of each bewitching bairn.

Air—A bonny young lad is my Jockey.

I'll sing to amuse you by night and by day,
And be unco merry when you are but gay;
When you with your bagpipes are ready to play,
My voice shall be ready to carol away
   With Sandy, and Sawney, and Jockey,
   With Sawney, and Jarvie, and Jockey.

MRS. BULKLEY.

Ye gamesters, who, so eager in pursuit,

Make but of all your fortune one *va toute:*
Ye jockey tribe, whose stock of words are few,
"I hold the odds.—Done, done, with you, with you."
Ye barristers, so fluent with grimace,
"My Lord,—your Lordship misconceives the case."
Doctors, who cough and answer every misfortuner,
"I wish I'd been called in a little sooner,"
Assist my cause with hands and voices hearty,
Come end the contest here, and aid my party.

MISS CATLEY.

Air—Ballinamony.

Ye brave Irish lads, hark away to the crack,
Assist me, I pray, in this woful attack;
For sure I don't wrong you, you seldom are slack,
When the ladies are calling, to blush, and hang back.
    For you're always polite and attentive,
    Still to amuse us inventive,
    And death is your only preventive:
       Your hands and your voices for me.

MRS. BULKLEY.

Well, Madam, what if, after all this sparring,
We both agree, like friends, to end our jarring?

MISS CATLEY.

And that our friendship may remain unbroken,
What if we leave the Epilogue unspoken?

MRS. BULKLEY.

Agreed.

MISS CATLEY.

    Agreed.

MRS. BULKLEY.

              And now with late repentance,
Un-epilogued the Poet waits his sentence.
Condemn the stubborn fool who can't submit
To thrive by flattery, though he starves by wit.

                                [*Exeunt.*

EPILOGUE [107]

THERE is a place, so Ariosto sings,
A treasury for lost and missing things;
Lost human wits have places there assign'd them,
And they, who lose their senses, there may find them.
But where's this place, this storehouse of the age?
The Moon, says he:—but *I* affirm the Stage:
At least in many things, I think, I see
His lunar and our mimic world agree.
Both shine at night, for, but at Foote's alone, [108]
We scarce exhibit till the sun goes down.
Both prone to change, no settled limits fix,
And sure the folks of both are lunatics.
But in this parallel my best pretence is,
That mortals visit both to find their senses.
To this strange spot, Rakes, Macaronies, Cits,
Come thronging to collect their scatter'd wits.
The gay coquette, who ogles all the day,
Comes here at night, and goes a prude away.
Hither the affected city dame advancing,
Who sighs for operas, and dotes on dancing,
Taught by our art her ridicule to pause on,
Quits the *Ballet*, and calls for *Nancy Dawson*.
The Gamester, too, whose wit's all high or low,
Oft risks his fortune on one desperate throw,
Comes here to saunter, having made his bets,
Finds his lost senses out, and pays his debts.
The Mohawk[109] too—with angry phrases stored,
As "Dam'me, Sir," and "Sir, I wear a sword;"

[107] This was first published in Percy's *Miscellaneous Works*
of Goldsmith, 1801, II. 87-88. Percy got it from Goldsmith himself.

[108] Foote gave morning performances. His *Piety in Patterns*
(see Introduction) was produced in this way on the 6th March,
1773.

[109] A species of midnight rake and ruffian of whom there is an
account by Budgell in *Spectator* No. 347. He belongs to Swift's,
rather than Goldsmith's day; but the race never dies out.

Here lesson'd for a while, and hence retreating,
Goes out, affronts his man, and takes a beating.
Here come the sons of scandal and of news,
But find no sense—for they had none to lose.
Of all the tribe here wanting an adviser
Our Author's the least likely to grow wiser;
Has he not seen how your favour place,
On sentimental Queens and Lords in lace?
Without a star, a coronet or garter,
How can the piece expect or hope for quarter?
No high-life scenes, no sentiment:—the creature
Still stoops among the low to copy nature.
Yes, he's far gone:—and yet some pity fix,
The English laws forbid to punish lunatics.

SONG

Intended to have been sung in "She Stoops to Conquer." [110]

Ah, me! when shall I marry me?
  Lovers are plenty; but fail to relieve me:
He, fond youth, that could carry me,
  Offers to love, but means to deceive me,

But I will rally, and combat the ruiner:
  Not a look, not a smile shall my passion discover:
She that gives all to the false one pursuing her,
  Makes but a penitent, loses a lover.

[110] This song was sent by Boswell to *The London Magazine* for June, 1774, with the following:—

'To the Editor of *The London Magazine*.

Sir,—I send you a small production of the late Dr. *Goldsmith*, which has never been published, and which might perhaps have been totally lost had I not secured it. He intended it as a song in the character of Miss *Hardcastle*, in his admirable comedy, *She Stoops to Conquer*; but it was left out, as Mrs. *Bulkley* who played the part did not sing. He sung it himself in private companies very agreeably. The tune is a pretty Irish air, called *The Humours of Balamagairy*, to which, he told me, he found it very difficult to adapt words; but he has succeeded very happily in these few lines. As I could sing the tune, and was fond of them, he was so good as to give me them about a year ago, just as I was leaving London, and bidding him adieu for that season, little apprehending that it was a last farewell. I preserve this little relick in his own handwriting with an affectionate care.

        I am, Sir,
            Your humble Servant,
                JAMES BOSWELL.'

DRAMABOOKS

PLAYS

MD 1 *Christopher Marlowe* (Tamburlaine the Great, Parts I & II, Doctor Faustus, The Jew of Malta, Edward the Second)
MD 2 *William Congreve* (Complete Plays)
MD 3 *Webster and Tourneur* (The White Devil, The Duchess of Malfi, The Atheist's Tragedy, The Revenger's Tragedy)
MD 4 *John Ford* (The Lover's Melancholy, 'Tis Pity She's a Whore, The Broken Heart, Love's Sacrifice, Perkin Warbeck)
MD 5 *Richard Brinsley Sheridan* (The Rivals, St. Patrick's Day, The Duenna, A Trip to Scarborough, The School for Scandal, The Critic)
MD 6 *Camille and Other Plays* (Scribe: A Peculiar Position, The Glass of Water; Sardou: A Scrap of Paper; Dumas: Camille; Augier: Olympe's Marriage)
MD 7 *John Dryden* (The Conquest of Granada, Parts I & II, Marriage à la Mode, Aureng-Zebe)
MD 8 *Ben Jonson* Vol. 1 (Volpone, Epicoene, The Alchemist)
MD 9 *Oliver Goldsmith* (The Good Natur'd Man, She Stoops to Conquer, An Essay on the Theatre, A Register of Scotch Marriages)
MD 10 *Jean Anouilh* Vol. 1 (Antigone, Eurydice, The Rehearsal, Romeo and Jeannette, The Ermine)
MD 11 *Let's Get a Divorce! and Other Plays* (Labiche: A Trip Abroad, and Célimare; Sardou: Let's Get a Divorce!; Courteline: These Cornfields; Feydeau: Keep an Eye on Amélie; Prévert: A United Family; Achard: Essay on Feydeau)
MD 12 *Jean Giraudoux* Vol. 1 (Ondine, The Enchanted, The Madwoman of Chaillot, The Apollo of Bellac)
MD 13 *Jean Anouilh* Vol. 2 (Restless Heart, Time Remembered, Ardèle, Mademoiselle Colombe, The Lark)
MD 14 *Henrik Ibsen: The Last Plays* (Little Eyolf, John Gabriel Borkman, When We Dead Awaken)
MD 15 *Ivan Turgenev* (A Month in the Country, A Provincial Lady, A Poor Gentleman)
MD 16 *George Farquhar* (The Constant Couple, The Twin-Rivals, The Recruiting Officer, The Beaux' Stratagem)
MD 17 *Jean Racine* (Andromache, Britannicus, Berenice, Phaedra, Athaliah)
MD 18 *The Storm and Other Russian Plays* (The Storm, The Government Inspector, The Power of Darkness, Uncle Vanya, The Lower Depths)
MD 19 *Michel de Ghelderode: Seven Plays* Vol. 1 (The Ostend Interviews, Chronicles of Hell, Barabbas, The Women at the Tomb, Pantagleize, The Blind Men, Three Players and a Play, Lord Halewyn)
MD 20 *Lope de Vega: Five Plays* (Peribáñez, Fuenteovejuna, The Dog in the Manger, The Knight from Olmedo, Justice Without Revenge)
MD 21 *Calderón: Four Plays* (Secret Vengeance for Secret Insult, Devotion to the Cross, The Mayor of Zalamea, The Phantom Lady)
MD 22 *Jean Cocteau: Five Plays* (Orphée, Antigone, Intimate Relations, The Holy Terrors, The Eagle with Two Heads)
MD 23 *Ben Jonson* Vol. 2 (Every Man in His Humour, Sejanus, Bartholomew Fair)
MD 24 *Port-Royal and Other Plays* (Claudel: Tobias and Sara; Mauriac: Asmodée; Copeau: The Poor Little Man; Montherlant: Port-Royal)
MD 25 *Edwardian Plays* (Maugham: Loaves and Fishes; Hankin: The Return of the Prodigal; Shaw: Getting Married; Pinero: Mid-Channel; Granville-Barker: The Madras House)
MD 26 *Alfred de Musset: Seven Plays*
MD 27 *Georg Büchner: Complete Plays and Prose*
MD 28 *Paul Green: Five Plays* (Johnny Johnson, In Abraham's Bosom, Hymn to the Rising Sun, The House of Connelly, White Dresses)
MD 29 *François Billetdoux: Two Plays* (Tchin-Tchin, Chez Torpe)
MD 30 *Michel de Ghelderode: Seven Plays* Vol. 2 (Red Magic, Hop, Signor!, The Death of Doctor Faust, Christopher Columbus, A Night of Pity, Piet Bouteille, Miss Jairus)
MD 31 *Jean Giraudoux* Vol. 2 (Siegfried, Amphitryon 38, Electra)
MD 32 *Kelly's Eye and Other Plays* by Henry Livings (Kelly's Eye, Big Soft Nellie, There's No Room for You Here for a Start)
MD 33 *Gabriel Marcel: Three Plays* (A Man of God, Ariadne, The Votive Candle)
MD 34 *New American Plays* Vol. 1, ed. by Robert W. Corrigan
MD 35 *Elmer Rice: Three Plays* (The Adding Machine, Street Scene, Dream Girl)
MD 36 *The Day the Whores Came Out to Play Tennis . . .* by Arthur Kopit
MD 37 *Platonov* by Anton Chekhov
MD 38 *Ugo Betti: Three Plays* (The Inquiry, Goat Island, The Gambler)
MD 39 *Jean Anouilh* Vol. 3 (Thieves' Carnival, Medea, Cécile, Traveler Without

Luggage, Orchestra, Episode in the Life of an Author, Catch As Catch Can)
MD 40 *Max Frisch: Three Plays* (Don Juan, The Great Rage of Philip Hotz, When the War Was Over)
MD 41 *New American Plays* Vol. 2 ed. by William M. Hoffman
MD 42 *Plays from Black Africa* ed. by Fredric M. Litto
MD 101 *Bussy D'Ambois* by George Chapman
MD 102 *The Broken Heart* by John Ford
MD 103 *The Duchess of Malfi* by John Webster
MD 104 *Doctor Faustus* by Christopher Marlowe
MD 105 *The Alchemist* by Ben Jonson
MD 106 *The Jew of Malta* by Christopher Marlowe
MD 107 *The Revenger's Tragedy* by Cyril Tourneur
MD 108 *A Game at Chess* by Thomas Middleton
MD 109 *Every Man in His Humour* by Ben Jonson
MD 110 *The White Devil* by John Webster
MD 111 *Edward the Second* by Christopher Marlowe
SD 1 *The Last Days of Lincoln* by Mark Van Doren
SD 2 *Oh Dad, Poor Dad . . .* by Arthur Kopit
SD 3 *The Chinese Wall* by Max Frisch
SD 4 *Billy Budd* by Louis O. Coxe and Robert Chapman
SD 5 *The Devils* by John Whiting
SD 6 *The Firebugs* by Max Frisch
SD 7 *Andorra* by Max Frisch
SD 8 *Balm in Gilead and Other Plays* by Lanford Wilson
SD 9 *Matty and the Moron and Madonna* by Herbert Lieberman
SD 10 *The Brig* by Kenneth H. Brown
SD 11 *The Cavern* by Jean Anouilh
SD 12 *Saved* by Edward Bond
SD 13 *Eh?* by Henry Livings
SD 14 *The Rimers of Eldritch and Other Plays* by Lanford Wilson
SD 16 *Ergo* by Jakov Lind

CRITICISM

D 1 *Shakespeare and the Elizabethans* by Henri Fluchère
D 2 *On Dramatic Method* by Harley Granville-Barker
D 3 *George Bernard Shaw* by G. K. Chesterton
D 4 *Paradox of Acting* by Diderot and *Masks or Faces?* by William Archer
D 5 *The Scenic Art* by Henry James
D 7 *Hazlitt on Theatre* ed. by William Archer and Robert Lowe
D 8 *The Fervent Years* by Harold Clurman
D 9 *The Quintessence of Ibsenism* by Bernard Shaw
D 10 *Papers on Playmaking* ed. by Brander Matthews
D 11 *Papers on Acting* ed. by Brander Matthews
D 12 *The Theatre* by Stark Young
D 13 *Immortal Shadows* by Stark Young
D 14 *Shakespeare: A Survey* by E. K. Chambers
D 15 *The English Dramatic Critics* ed. by James Agate
D 16 *Japanese Theatre* by Faubion Bowers
D 17 *Shaw's Dramatic Criticism* (1895-98) ed. by John F. Matthews
D 18 *Shaw on Theatre* ed. by E. J. West
D 19 *The Book of Job as a Greek Tragedy* by Horace Meyer Kallen
D 20 *Molière: The Man Seen Through the Plays* by Ramon Fernandez
D 21 *Greek Tragedy* by Gilbert Norwood
D 22 *Samuel Johnson on Shakespeare* ed. by W. K. Wimsatt, Jr.
D 23 *The Poet in the Theatre* by Ronald Peacock
D 24 *Chekhov the Dramatist* by David Magarshack
D 25 *Theory and Technique of Playwriting* by John Howard Lawson
D 26 *The Art of the Theatre* by Henri Ghéon
D 27 *Aristotle's Poetics* with an Introduction by Francis Fergusson
D 28 *The Origin of the Theater* by Benjamin Hunningher
D 29 *Playwrights on Playwriting* by Toby Cole
D 30 *The Sense of Shakespeare's Sonnets* by Edward Hubler
D 31 *The Development of Shakespeare's Imagery* by Wolfgang Clemen
D 32 *Stanislavsky on the Art of the Stage* trans. by David Magershack
D 33 *Metatheatre: A New View of Dramatic Form* by Lionel Abel
D 34 *The Seven Ages of the Theatre* by Richard Southern
D 35 *The Death of Tragedy* by George Steiner
D 36 *Greek Comedy* by Gilbert Norwood
D 37 *Ibsen: Letters and Speeches* ed. by Evert Sprinchorn
D 38 *The Testament of Samuel Beckett* by J. Jacobsen and W. R. Mueller
D 39 *On Racine* by Roland Barthes
D 40 *American Playwrights on Drama* ed. by Horst Frenz
D 41 *How Shakespeare Spent the Day* by Ivor Brown
D 42 *Brecht on Theatre* ed. by John Willett
D 43 *Costume in the Theatre* by James Laver
D 44 *Ionesco and Genet* by J. Jacobsen and W. R. Mueller
D 45 *Commedia dell'Arte* by Giacomo Oreglia